Timothy Regan

Ghost Towns of
NEW JERSEY

A Tour of Our Forgotten Places

Schiffer Publishing Ltd

4880 Lower Valley Road • Atglen, PA 19310

THIS BOOK IS DEDICATED TO MY DAUGHTER,
ELIZABETH ANN, WHO IS OUR FAMILY'S
TRAVELING PARTNER, FELLOW EXPLORER, AND
PHOTOGRAPHER. WE LOVE YOU!

AND TO:
THE MEN AND WOMEN OF THE NEW JERSEY
FOREST FIRE SERVICE WHO HAVE PROTECTED AND
PRESERVED THE TOWNS AND VILLAGES IN THIS
BOOK SINCE 1906. THANK YOU AND BE SAFE.

CONTENTS

FOREWORD

Ghost Towns of New Jersey: A Tour of Our Forgotten Places represents more than a dozen lost and forgotten communities throughout our state where these forges, furnaces, and company towns once served as agricultural and transportation hubs in their heyday. As the years passed, these vibrant places, once full of color and life, slowly slipped into obscurity and disappeared as places people once called home. Nearly all of the locations in the pages of this book faced significant threats from wildfires and floods on a pretty regular basis; fires themselves posed the biggest risk, and as you read on, it was a calamity when the word "fire" was shouted out in the village streets. Of course, it wasn't just fire that spelled the end to some towns: changes in the economy, more modern production methods, or even bankruptcy put an end to these towns for good. Places like Allaire's Howell Works, relying solely on the bog iron methods, suffered economic distress after the market for bog iron dried up and no other industry was found to take its place.

New Jersey has a long history of large and deadly wildfires; recorded fires are known to have swept through good portions of the state many times. One such account, from 1755, reports a fire over thirty miles long between Barnegat and Little Egg Harbor.

In 1895, John Gifford reported to the state geologist that forty-nine fires burned 60,000 acres in Burlington, Atlantic, and Ocean counties. All of these threatened the historic villages, with the Town of Harrisville being completely consumed in a 1914 blaze. In the eighteenth and nineteenth centuries, countless other fires damaged places with nearly all of Batsto being destroyed in an 1874 fire, caused from a spark from John Stewart's chimney. Of course, there was little organized fire protection in these small communities; even with bucket brigades in place it is a wonder that any of them survived. Towns like Walpack, Flatbrookville, and Long Pond all suffered from severe river flooding that helped lead to their demise through two major reservoir projects. The Village of Round Valley in Hunterdon County was abandoned for that same-named reservoir in 1959, while the Monksville reservoir's own waters cover that once-proud town.

I have become familiar with many of these places throughout my career while listening to others talk about the former towns like Martha, Quaker Bridge, Pleasant Mills, or Bulltown that are well known to the Forest Fire Service. Some of these ghost towns may just be a few dots on a topographical map, or at an intersection deep in the woods roads,

or a place name that one of our firetower observers uses to give directions to our people and planes. Since wildfires were a constant threat to the livelihoods of the towns, many had an elevated area to look out for approaching wildfires. The Batsto Mansion Cupola was used to lookout for any wildfires that could approach the village starting in 1878. The ghost towns in the Delaware Water Gap, Waterloo Village, and Long Pond, continue to face a threat of wildfires and rely upon our firetowers to spot small fires before they can grow to conflagrations.

The New Jersey Forest Fire Service is proud to have contributed in a small way to the protection of these places, many of which belong to the people of New Jersey as part of our State Parks.

So, please enjoy this fantastic journey through New Jersey as we explore these wonderful and unique Jersey ghost towns, and please be careful with fire out there; it is up to all of us to do our part to prevent wildfires.

John H. Reith
Asst. Fire Warden
Division B
NJ State Forest Fire Service

Overall State Ghost Town Map

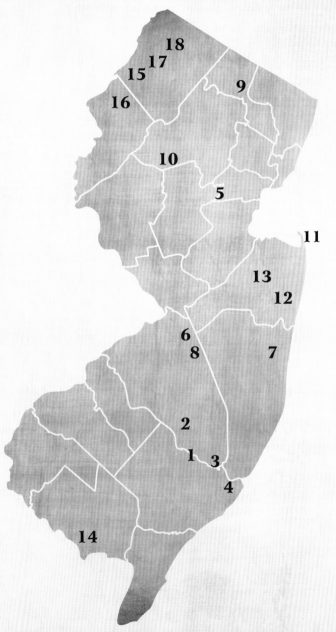

1. Batsto

2. Atsion

3. Pleasant Mills

4. Chestnut Neck

5. Feltville

6. Smithville

7. Double Trouble

8. Whitesbog

9. Long Pond

10. Waterloo

11. Sandy Hook

12. Allaire

13. Phalanx

14. Greenwich

15. Flatbookville

16. Millbrook

17. Walpack Center

18. Bevans

PREFACE

Do the words "ghost town" bring images of dust blowing down a deserted Main Street with the sound of a lonesome unlatched shutter banging in the wind intrigue you? Well, if it does, then step inside these pages, for our journey is about to begin. We will visit eighteen towns that were born, prospered, and then faded away into history. Most of them have slipped away completely, some have been preserved, and a few still barely cling to life.

Our Jersey ghost towns are to be found in every part of the Garden State—from the mountains of Sussex County to the salt marshes of Cumberland County—while some of our beloved towns remain today in state and county parks, tucked along quiet country roads and sometimes way off that dusty country lane. To truly experience these special places from our past, let us look back in time; it is a trip you will want to take again and again.

ACKNOWLEDGMENTS

No one person has ever successfully researched or completed a book of any size or subject without the help of a few others. In a book of this scope and complexity, spanning from one end of New Jersey to the other, I have many to thank for helping, guiding, suggesting, and providing information that made it complete. Foremost my thanks to my wife, Patti, who has assisted me with all of my publications for over twenty years; it is her watchful eye as a teacher that keeps my grammar straight and my writing sensible. To our daughter, Elizabeth, who has been taking these journeys with us since she was born, I will take her lack of complaining as encouragement that she enjoys all these trips just a little bit. To my brother, Dan, whose childhood trips will never be forgotten or your requests for minibikes, pocketknives, etc., that added fun to the backseat life. To my mother-in-law, Linda Schleicher, for everything. My lifelong friends who always support my projects: Dave Galloway, Jimmy McTernan, Randy Stout, and John Reith.

Thanks to my Sandy Hook contingent; Rob Louden, Frank DeLuca, Bruce Lane, C. J. Gutch, Maren Morsch, Larry Winchell, Brian Malley, Shawn Miller, Scott Shanker, Mike Thomas, Mark Christiano, and last but not least Park Historian Tom Hoffman. Mike Thomson. My brothers at NWS Earle Fire Department, Ben Brick of J. R. Brick Company; Alicia M. Bjornson, Historian Batsto Village; retired NJ State Rangers, Gary Baumgartner and Joanne Christos; Shawn Judy NJFFS; the members of the Walpack Twp Historical Society for their kindness and photos; Jen Wycalek and Myra Snook; Eric Orange, Burlington County Parks Historian; my Keyport family, Bert Morris, Les Horner, Bert Aumack, Jack and Angel Jeandron, the late Al and Faye Bennett. Emile Schettino, for his many miles as co-pilot. Of course, I would be remiss if I left out the Mississippi contingent, Hank and Karen Levins, Gary Joffrion, and Sean Barna, and to all of the others who made this book rise from an idea to the bookstores, a sincere thank you.

Off the beaten path.

INTRODUCTION

I'm sure that my quest for these abandoned places began the same way as many of yours did: school trips to Allaire or Batsto, weekend getaways with our families, or just thumbing through the pages of a book like Becks' *Forgotten Towns of Southern Jersey,* which has ignited countless weekend explorers of forgotten New Jersey for nearly a century.

Our state holds a magnificent variety of ghost towns in every region; one not need travel very far to find one of these places tucked away on a sandy road in the pines or along a densely forested mountain road. Places like Long Pond Ironworks, Walpack Center, Feltville, and Atsion, all filled with broken dreams and lost fortunes that now hold secrets for us to discover—and often mysteries waiting to be solved. Conducting research on the history of one community is work, on a county it is a commitment, and putting it all together on eighteen different villages in nine counties is a challenge. My original plan was to include all of the places that would be of interest to you; however, it became impractical without having a 400-page book. My regrets for not including Harrisville in Burlington County, but the lack of historic photographs and difficulty in photographing ruins forced me to set it aside for now—it is, however, a place well worth visiting. At least two dozen other places were also worthy to have been

included: some are Fries Mills in Cumberland County, Estelleville in Atlantic, Hermann City in Burlington, and so many others scattered near your towns. Two reconstructed sites, Smithville in Atlantic County and Cold Spring Village in Cape May are made up mostly of buildings from other locations and were not included; both are also great day trips. As with the research of any book, you get to meet people from all over who share your same passion for our state's history, and it's always an exciting moment when that occurs. My apologies for any inaccuracies that you may come across. With nearly every ghost town combined here I researched around 1,600 years of history, something was bound to have wound up missing.

Many of these places are steeped in the very foundation of our nation's battle for independence. The iron furnaces and the towns that sprung up around them, their production of cannonballs, shot, and other iron supplies for the Continental Army were crucial in helping win our freedom from England. The very place of New Jersey's famed Tea Party of 1774 today lies abandoned and almost forgotten along the ancient Cohansey Creek in the sleepy Colonial village of Greenwich.

Ghost Towns of New Jersey is a journey to the glass towns, romantic iron furnace villages, and sleepy hamlets that have simply

A window into our past.

faded away from our memories over the centuries. We in New Jersey have the luxury to drive, hike, and even canoe to these places, all within an hour or two of home—some on the road, some off the road, and some way off the beaten path and through the thorny thickets. But any way you choose to get there, those Jersey ghost towns are waiting for you to explore and enjoy. Of course always take a moment to remember those souls who once filled these places with life.

Overall State Ghost Town Map

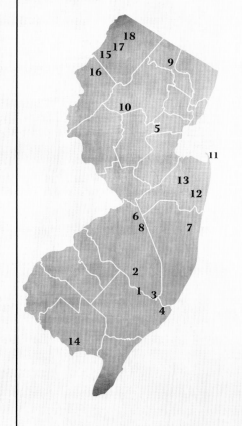

1. Batsto
2. Atsion
3. Pleasant Mills
4. Chestnut Neck
5. Feltville
6. Smithville
7. Double Trouble
8. Whitesbog
9. Long Pond
10. Waterloo
11. Sandy Hook
12. Allaire
13. Phalanx
14. Greenwich
15. Flatbookville
16. Millbrook
17. Walpack Center
18. Bevans

THE JERSEY DEVIL
Born 1735

Like all good legends, the story of the Jersey Devil is shrouded in a mix of fact, fiction, and some plain ol' storytelling. Although there are at least a half dozen accounts of the formation of this winged creature that haunts the southern half of the state, what follows is the most recorded of the tales. It appears that the creature was born to a woman known as Mother Leeds in the year 1735. Ma Leeds already had twelve children and, as the story goes, was not embracing the birth of the thirteenth child. Upon becoming pregnant, she exclaimed, "Let the Devil have it!" And that was all she needed to say.

So, as a furious thunderstorm rolled into the Leeds Point area, Mother Leeds was about to give birth, with a midwife nearby and other family members in the house. A baby boy was delivered around midnight on a day and time that have been long forgotten—if they ever existed at all. The baby boy was perfectly normal and healthy upon being cleaned by the midwife and handed over to his mother . . . only as everyone watched, the tiny baby boy transformed into a cloven-hoofed beast with the head of a collie, the snout of a horse, and the tail of a dragon!

From here the tale has a few variations; one is that he simply left through the chimney into the stormy Burlington County sky. Some say that he devoured everyone in the room before fleeing through a hole in the roof of the home.

In Henry Charlton Beck's book, *Jersey Genesis*, Beck interviewed a Mrs. Bowen in 1945. Bowen, whose family had lived in the Leeds Point area for centuries, swore to the story's truthfulness and took Beck to the exact spot where the Jersey Devil was born. It was in the ancient Shourds house, which was built prior to 1750, where the Leeds family lived, and the Devil was said to have been born into the folklore of New Jersey that stormy night.

The Jersey Devil, who often answers to the Leeds Devil, has been menacing the citizens of the great State since his birth. Throughout Atlantic, Cumberland, Burlington, Salem, Camden, and Cape May counties the Jersey Devil has appeared to over 2,000 people over

WANTED
by the Court of Burlington
for treacherous Actiofs

A general description of the beast from J. Leeds

A Devil Like creature born to Mother Leeds of this Vicinity as of late last Tuesday Eve'ning during the late Nor'easter
The creature has caused much destruction and the killing of several prized animals, it is considered dangerous and should be dispatched if at all possible
Oct 31. 1735
10 Guinea Reward upon bringing the Beast to the Sheriff

the years. Along his path are mutilated farm animals, (he appears to really enjoy chicken) and occasionally missing dogs and cats. Hysteria throughout the Gibbstown area, in 1951, caused the intervention of local and state police to calm the folks down after the Devil was sighted in a window by a twelve-year-old boy. Though the boy stuck to his story, his siblings seemed to think he dreamed the whole ordeal up.

The ancient Shourds House collapsed by the 1950s and is nearly impossible to find today in the Leeds Point Area. The Devil's other birthplace, the Jersey ghost town of Estelleville, has nearly vanished as well with only a few brick archways and walls remaining today. The Devil once made an appearance in the television show *X-Files* where the show's two agents tried tracking the beast through the Pine Barrens with the help of a state ranger.

Continued efforts to capture, corral, photograph, and otherwise track the Devil have been highly unsuccessful over the years, although his footprints have been discovered throughout the Pine Barrens, and his shrieks still send terror through those who believe!

A wanted poster demanding the capture of the Jersey Devil most likely was circulated many times during the centuries of its reported sightings. The Devil himself has been a staple of New Jersey folklore for over five centuries, and somewhere, somehow, its origins are most likely based on some facts deeply hidden in the history of the Leeds Point Area.

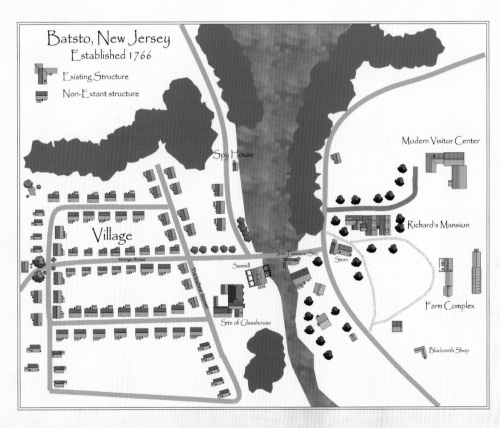

Batsto, New Jersey
Established 1766

Existing Structure

Non-Extant structure

Spy House

Village

Bridge Street

Buckshutem Street

Sawmill

Iron Furnace Site

Site of Glasshouse

Modern Visitor Center

Richard's Mansion

Store

Farm Complex

Blacksmith Shop

The Village of Batsto lies deep in the heart of the Pine Barrens tucked within the vast expanse of Wharton State Forest in southeastern Burlington County. Batsto takes its name from the Scandinavian name of "badstu," which means bathing place. Like many of the other communities in this book, Batsto was settled around the site of a Colonial Iron Furnace. While still under English rule, Israel Pemberton assumed management of the furnace site and is considered to be the first to have built many of the original structures there, including the manor house, which he named Whitcomb Manor. He had all but completed this initial construction by 1766. In just a few short years, Pemberton sold out the property to Charles Read, who enlarged the bog iron and smelting furnace along the banks of the Mullica River. Read's bog iron industry and furnace became the largest in South Jersey, and by the dawn of the American Revolution, the ironworks was producing iron and casting housewares, as well as cannonballs and shot for the Continental Army. Throughout the American Revolution, Batsto was a key industry in the supply chain for Washington. So vital was this place that, in 1778, the British were heading to capture and destroy Batsto's Ironworks when they attacked and destroyed the Village of Chestnut Neck. The quick action of a small group of volunteer militia turned back the advancing British troops, sparing the village of Batsto, ensuring Continental troops would have supplies to win the war.

One question that surfaced over time was exactly how the British commanders knew of Batsto and its exact location: Loyalist spies, that is how! From the very Village of Batsto itself, along old Bank Street, was the home of a villager, and Loyalist in secret, whose home overlooked the furnace operation and supply wagons. It is assumed that he interacted with the workers and villagers, perhaps even working there, reporting back detailed lists of munitions to William Tryon, a staunch Loyalist and British citizen who was then serving as Governor of New York. It is not known what eventually happened to the Batsto Loyalist; however, the Spy House that stands today may not be the original one overlooking Batsto Lake, as it was discovered during a 1960s archaeology survey that the dwelling dated to only about 1812.

After the Revolution, Batsto continued to prosper as an iron making village and unlike Martha Furnace, Etna Furnace, and others, it flourished, reaching a peak population of about 500 citizens by 1830. In 1784, William Richards took ownership of the works, and the foundry was well known for its fine rust resistant pig iron, quality hinges and nails, as well as window sash weights and other items.

Exactly how did Batsto's iron ever make it out of this desolate village? Today, the village seems far off from the Atlantic Ocean, and visitors might wonder how ocean-going ships received Batsto's wares. In the eighteenth and nineteenth centuries, the Mullica River from Chestnut Neck to the Forks beyond Green Bank was a deep navigable waterway where large sailing ships could come within a half-mile of Batsto Landing where, then, small skiffs could be taken

The famed "Spy House" of Batsto is shown here during a 1935 Historic American Buildings Survey photograph. The house was alleged for centuries to have been home to a Loyalist who spied and reported back to General Clinton about the daily happenings at Batsto. After much research it seems this building was completed around 1812, perhaps on the foundation of the actual Spy House. (The Library of Congress)

The actual origins of the Batsto Ironmasters houses remain a much-debated subject. It is thought that the original two-and one-story sections were completed by Israel Pemberton and named Whitcomb Manor. This image shows the large two-story addition with typical federal style stepped eaves that was built by William Richards between 1790 and 1800. (State of New Jersey Archives)

to meet the ships and off-load to the larger vessels. In 1956, one of these skiffs was found in the Batsto Lake; it is today on display in the village. Most of the overland routes would have taken the Cooper Ferry Road, which was a deeply forested forty-mile trip that went straight to the present Camden City wharfs along the Delaware.

By 1825, the village consisted of a Manor House, gristmill, outbuildings, sawmill, and a series of seven gridded streets lined with over seventy neat whitewashed two-story clapboard homes. Among the streets of the town, in 1856, were Bridge, Oak, Water, Tuckahoe, and Lake Streets.

In 1809, William Richards, the imposing, kind owner of the works retired to Mount Holly and left the village and the industry to his son, Jesse.

An entire book could be written about Jesse Richards, his labors, and his love for his beloved Batsto. *Iron in the Pines* by Franklin Pierce and *Batsto Village* by Barbara Smith-Solem are excellent works for detailed insights into the life and times of the village.

As the ironmaster, he was mayor, judge, boss, and big brother to those who worked and lived in the community. Jesse and his wife, Sarah (Haskins), ran the big house and the village for nearly a half-century. Children were educated, grew, married, and started another generation all within Jesse's ownership of Batsto; it was a way of life for many and a good one at that. The houses were rented for a small amount monthly, with gardens behind each home to ensure that corn, tomatoes, watermelons, and every other Jersey crop could be grown in plenty while in season. The post office was commissioned in 1852 and would remain open fairly regularly until the close of the nineteenth century. Even before the bog iron industry moved west, Jesse knew that it was up to him to keep the village and his father's legacy alive at Batsto. By the mid 1840s, two glass houses had been built and were turning out hand blown window glass, streetlamp lenses, and other flat glass. The sounds of the sawmill were in constant earshot, and the lumber industry helped to keep food on the table during the times that both glassmaking and iron production waned. One constant threat to the glass house was fire; it was reported that by the Civil War, in 1863, fourteen separate fires had either damaged or destroyed the glass houses. It is believed

that during the 1860s, Batsto received a hand-operated fire engine for protection; however, it seems to have done little good when it was needed most, and no organized fire company was established to use it efficiently! Jesse continued to diversify Batsto's products, and from 1820 to 1850, the village had dabbled in the making of iron, glass, and bricks; shipbuilding served as a marketplace, stage stop, and a busy agricultural center. All of this was conducted under Richard's watchful eye.

In 1854, Jesse Richards died in the big house with Sarah by his side, and it was from that moment on that Batsto would never quite be the same. In 1858, the iron furnace was shut down for the final time and soon after torn down by the sons and grandsons of those who had built it nearly a century earlier. Iron had now been produced at the site for nearly one hundred years, long outliving the other iron furnaces throughout New Jersey. Richards was laid to rest in his beloved church cemetery under a large tomb that still reads: Honored, Respected, Mourned.

Third generation Richards family member and Jesse's son, Thomas, took over the operation of the place upon his father's death. It is said that Thomas was of good nature and caring heart but was not the businessman that his father and grandfather had been. Thomas continued to operate the glass house and lumbering industry, but the villages glory days had faded and, by 1868, had entered into receivership.

It was that fateful freezing night of February 23, 1874, that dealt the village its final blow. It seems that some sparks from Robert Stewart's (the village manager) house set fire to his neighbors dwelling; by dawn, seventeen homes had been destroyed. Both glass houses were a pile of smoking timbers, and the remains of the iron furnace had also been swallowed up in the fire. Many moved away, including Thomas Richards, and two years later, the village industries were silenced. Deep in debt, Batsto the Revolutionary town was sold at auction for just $14,000 to Philadelphia businessman Joseph Wharton.

Upon seeing the remains of Batsto, Wharton didn't know if he should rebuild or just tear the whole place down. Lucky for history he chose to rebuild. Within a few years, Wharton had completely modernized the ironmaster's house, or big house, rebuilt outbuildings, including the sawmill, and renovated many of the village homes, slowly shining up the ol' place. Wharton grew sugar beets and raised livestock; those who remained in the village found work once again, and for the next thirty-three years, the Wharton Empire ruled over 100,000 acres of the Pinelands. With his death in 1909, the Wharton Estate continued to manage the place, and although its industries mostly faded away, a few folks still called Batsto home for another eighty years.

Batsto for the day. One amazing fact that should be noted is that the last proud resident of Batsto remained living there until 1989, roughly 223 years after the first resident moved in, whom my Mom and I had the pleasure of meeting in the early 1980s.

Today the village remains a beautiful relic of a forgotten time, worth the visit any time of year, and when you stroll around those ancient buildings, give a thought or two of Jesse and Sarah who just might be strolling a bit behind you, just out of view in the rustling leaves.

BATSTO TODAY

The year 1954 saw the entire Wharton Estate purchased by the State of New Jersey as protected forest. With this purchase came along all of the secrets and ghost towns of the Wharton Estate; Atsion, Martha, Batsto, Washington, Harrisville, and many others that would now be able to be explored and protected for the future.

Restoration began in 1955, with the big house, post office-store, and sawmill being the first to receive taxpayer monies for the process. By 1959, the new Park Visitor Center was dedicated and when built resembled an early nineteenth-century structure; within twenty years it would be tripled in size being reincarnated into a large modern building, looking a bit out of place at the village entrance.

During the 1960s, the village restorations continued, and the Batsto Citizens Committee, which was created when the park was established, worked hard to guide the renovations and supplied the love to the labor to make it work. One of the highlights of the restoration work was the rededication of the Batsto Post Office in its original location in 1966. Throughout the 1960s costumed interpreters roamed the village streets as the farm wagon and stagecoaches plied through the landscape full of families and history buffs who went to

Visitor Information

Batsto Village is today part of the expansive Wharton State Forest located along County Road 542, in Washington Twp (or Hammonton, NJ, for the GPS). The 1,200 acres of the village is open seven days a week, 365 days a year, from dawn to dusk. The park may be closed throughout the year for inclement weather, hunting, or prescribed burning, so I recommend calling the park office at 690-561-0024 before visiting. There are no concessions at the park, except for perhaps an occasional hot dog cart or Italian water ice stand, so come prepared with water and grub, and like the rest of New Jersey, the village gets very hot during the summer months with only the Visitor Center (open 9-4 p.m. daily) for respite. For lunch or dinner, driving ten minutes into Hammonton offers every food choice one could want.

Most of the workers houses in the village were single-family homes with rear-attached kitchens added before the Civil War. At one time, twelve double houses, such as this one, existed. Today, only three remain on the edge of Bridge Street and were restored by the State of New Jersey in the 1950s.

Among the most photographed Batsto buildings are the grist mill and corn crib. The current grist mill was completed in 1828 by Jesse Richards and may have been built upon the foundation of the original 1783 mill. The mill was restored and rededicated on June 25, 1967, and is still fully operational as it nears its 200th birthday. It can still produce a variety of milled flours when operating. The adjacent corn crib was completed around 1880.

Batsto's historic stagecoach mostly sits idle today after over forty years of being used for village tours. Constructed sometime in the middle of the nineteenth century this mostly original stagecoach once plied the sandy roads of the Pines, between the shore and Philadelphia. Once painted bright yellow, it is today an aging shade of red.

This view captures a good portion of the remaining farm and industrial buildings at the village. From left to right are: a reconstructed storage building with the roof of the c. 1790 store; the Richards Mansion; the 1852 stone mule barn in the foreground; and the piggery complex and water tower built around 1830 followed by a portion of the wagon sheds. Finally, the last buildings hold the blacksmith and wheelwright shops. These structures were built c. 1850 near the forge and later moved to this site in the 1890s. All of these buildings have been restored and are open to the public.

Joseph Wharton was a Philadelphia Quaker born in 1826 to a fairly wealthy family. He was just twenty-four when this Daguerreotype was made. The life of Wharton is an amazing tale of his life: scientist, farmer, entrepreneur, Washington lobbyist, traveler, explorer. Wharton's life is best understood in the 1987 biography, *Joseph Wharton: Quaker Industrial Pioneer* by Willard Ross Yates. Had it not been for Wharton, Batsto would most likely be only a memory. (The Library of Congress)

The Big House as it was known at Batsto, received an extensive renovation by Joseph Wharton in 1880. Wharton expansively remodeled the interior of the house, moving rooms, adding staircases, and installing running water supplied from a 1,200-gallon water tank high above in the new eighty-four foot Victorian tower. When finished, the house was the tallest structure between Philadelphia and Cape May; its tower was used as a forest fire lookout for decades to give early warning to the citizens throughout the area.

Wharton's large family lived only seasonally in the mansion. Hosting travelers, accommodating businessmen, and entertaining family members required a lavishly furnished home and a large servant staff. Most of the servants lived in the home itself while some lived in other parts of the village. Wharton likely brought most of his servant staff from his Philadelphia mansion, Ontalauna, to Batsto each summer.

The Batsto Post Office received its commission from President Millard Fillmore in 1852. The structure that it occupied was most likely renovated for that purpose during that same year. The state historian and author, Arthur D. Pierce noted in 1957 that the actual Whitcomb Manor, built in the 1760s, might be this building. Architectural features of the building, such as its gambrel roof and brickwork, would lend support to this theory as it appears to be a typical Philadelphia rowhouse of the colonial time period.

Batsto's Great Fire of 1874 spared these workers' homes along Bridge Street only after a thankful wind shift. Completed in the 1820s by Jesse Richards, at least seventy-three of these two-and-one-half-story homes once lined the five primary streets of the village. Most contained a large kitchen and living area on the first floor, where a small staircase climbed to the second floor's two small bedrooms.

Here is the seldom-viewed rear of the grist mill. Tied up along the dock is a typical pig iron boat, known as a Durham boat. The Durham boats were the primary vessels that enabled the oreman to remove the deposits from the bogs and bring them to the furnace for smelting. An original Durham boat was found in the lake bed in the 1950s and is today on display in the village.

New Jersey's forty-fifth governor, Richard M. Hughes, dedicated the new Batsto Visitor Center on May 15, 1964. This building, which has been extensively remodeled since then, bears little resemblance to the original. Hundreds of thousands of people have passed through these doors that serve as the Gateway to Batsto. Today, an extensive bookstore, first class museum, theater, and information desk are staffed by volunteers and State employees daily.

For a generation of students in New Jersey and Eastern Pennsylvania, the Batsto Stage ride was the highlight of their visit. For those of us lucky enough to have experienced Batsto in its heyday, climbing into the stage on a hot August weekend made for memories that will last a lifetime. The stagecoach itself was typical of those that plied the sand roads of the Pines and all across America throughout much of the country's first 120 years of existence.

Welcome to

PLEASANT MILLS

c. 1750

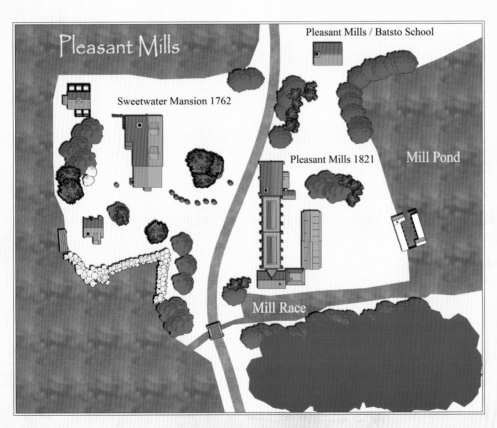

Pleasant Mills

Pleasant Mills / Batsto School

Sweetwater Mansion 1762

Pleasant Mills 1821

Mill Pond

Mill Race

MULLICA TWP, BURLINGTON COUNTY

The area known as the Forks had been part of the lands of an ancient Leni Lenape Village called Nescochague. The Lenape would pass through this area in the summer months to fish and live as they had done for centuries. Of course, it would not be long before the first white families arrived here and called the place home; among those were the Wescoats, Baxters, MacGillams, Pecks, and the Campbells, all Scottish Quakers who were searching for a new home in a new world. It was here where Jack Mullin constructed a sawmill in 1750, followed by a variety of industries beginning in the first quarter of the eighteenth century. It was also here during the Revolution that many ships were built, supplies were shipped from Batsto, and the river was lined with the comings and goings of a fledgling hopeful new Republic. It was not uncommon for a dozen or so sailing ships to be leaving for the West Indies, New York, and Philadelphia along the wharves on this part of the Mullica River.

The Forks actually appear to encompass a fairly larger area, extending from Batsto until it meets with the Village of Green Bank a few miles down the river. Eventually, the Forks broke up into smaller villages, such as Sweetwater and Crowleytown, both within a mile or two of each other. In 1762, a wealthy gentlemen by the name of Reid arrived from one of the sloops that once made the Forks her port; he fell in love with the place and soon erected a lavish home along the banks of Lake Nescochague. He named the colonial mansion Sweetwater, and soon the community surrounding it became known as the same. Sweetwater and Batsto was the setting for the 1855 Charles J. Peterson's romance novel *Kate Aylesford*, a story set during the American Revolution. In 1873, the book was re-released as *The Heiress of Sweetwater*. Today only a few original copies are known to exist, but it has been reprinted in recent years to the delight of many. Although the novel is based on a fictional character, most historians agree that Reid's own daughter, Honoria Reid, born about 1764 in Sweetwater, was the true inspiration for the novel's heroine.

By 1822, William Lippincott had built a stone cotton mill directly across the street from Sweetwater. Lippincott, who was the ironmaster of Batsto's brother-in-law, named the place the Pleasant Mills of Sweetwater. The old stone mill was the scene of at least two disastrous fires—one in 1856 and another in 1878.

Today, the quiet roads around the Forks, Sweetwater, or even Pleasant Mills seem to be a million miles away from the crowds of the Jersey Shore and the Garden State Parkway. Sweetwater still lies along the banks of Lake Nescochague, just as it has since 1762, while the Pleasant Mills School exists today as a house just to the northwest of the mill.

At the intersection of Nesco Road is the white frame church constructed by William Richards in 1808; the church has remained unchanged for over 200 years, and its graveyard holds the remains of those who built, lived, and loved in the area of the Forks.

Colonel Elijah Clark was born along the banks of the Mullica River in a long-forgotten town known as Clark's Landing in 1730. A well educated, prosperous young man, he settled in the ancient Nescochague Indian Village in 1757. He went about building this colonial mansion for his new bride, Jane, in 1762. He named the mansion Sweetwater. The sturdy structure has only been slightly modernized since it was built and was made famous in the 1855, historical romance novel *Kate Aylesford* by Charles J. Peterson. Clark died on December 9, 1795, with his beloved wife following him in 1804; both are buried in Woodbury.

Visitor Information

Pleasant Mills is not a park, so be careful parking if you plan on walking along County Road 643 or when taking photographs—no sidewalks and fast-moving Jersey drivers make for a rather interesting time! All buildings are private here so please respect that. You can easily visit Batsto, the Pleasant Mills Church, Pleasant Mills Village, and the site of St. Mary's church and cemetery.

Nearby, in the old churchyard, is the grave of Jesse's beloved wife, Sara Ennals Haskins. Jesse met Sarah after her minister father married Jesse's sister, Elizabeth, around 1805. They spent their life at Batsto raising three boys and three girls. The couple was married in the church at Pleasant Mills in about 1812; Sarah joined Jesse again on October 14, 1868.

It was on this site in 1762, that Colonel Clark built the second church in the area, known as Clarks Little Log Meeting house, which replaced an earlier one built by the Swedes in 1685. This church was completed in 1808 on the site of the previous log church and has been the area's gathering spot for worship for over 200 years.

Pleasant Mills had been so named after the early mills along the Nescochague Creek beginning in the eighteenth century. The new Pleasant Mills was an actual cotton mill built by William Lippincott in 1821. At this time it was named the Pleasant Mills at Sweetwater, which, along with Batsto and The Forks, made up the areas' communities. The Mill burned in 1834, burned again in 1855, and yet again in 1878. The walls of the old place are original, and for several years it operated as a theater. It has today fallen into ruins.

Jesse Richards from the second generation of the Richards family died at home on June 17th 1854. Jesse built Batsto into the thriving commercial and manufacturing center of the Pines and had lived near there his entire life. This large obelisk was carved in Mount Holly and placed upon his grave on October 25, 1854.

Welcome to
CHESTNUT NECK
c. 1750 Destroyed by the British 1778

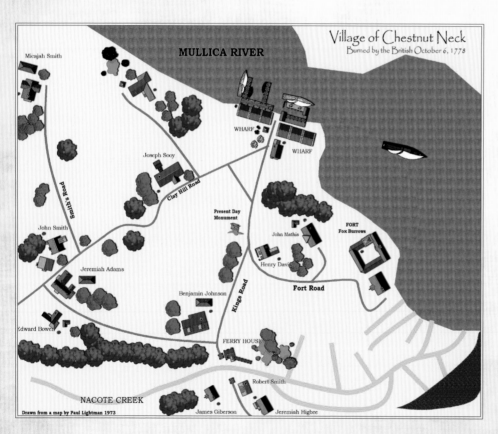

Village of Chestnut Neck
Burned by the British October 6, 1778

MULLICA RIVER

Micajah Smith

WHARF

WHARF

Joseph Sooy

Smith's Road

Clay Hill Road

Present Day Monument

FORT Fox Burrows

John Smith

John Mathis

Henry Davis

Jeremiah Adams

Benjamin Johnson

Kings Road

Fort Road

Edward Bowen

FERRY HOUSE

Robert Smith

NACOTE CREEK

Drawn from a map by Paul Lightman 1973

James Giberson   Jeremiah Higbee

PORT REPUBLIC, ATLANTIC COUNTY

One of Jersey's least known ghost towns is the village of Chestnut Neck, located off the Garden State Parkway at the point where the Mullica River heads towards Batsto from the Great Bay. Chestnut Neck hasn't been much of a location since 1778, when a band of British Naval marauders destroyed the majority of the place—but its story is incredible.

It was here on a small point of land between the Mullica River (then known as the Egg Harbor River) and the Nacote Creek that a village sprung up about 1770. Named Chestnut Neck, the new village was soon comprised of merchants and seamen, farmers and inn keepers, and of course, those privateers who became quite a thorn in the side of Loyalists. During this time, it was common practice for a government to issue a letter of marquee. This was a government license authorizing a person (who then became a privateer) to attack and capture enemy vessels, which could then be sold for profit. Privateers had been commissioned by colonial authorities, in 1774, to more or less harass, intimidate, and take possession of British ships; of course, they often protected patriot shipping vessels and provided escorts when needed as well. Over 400 of these privateers operated from the Raritan Bay to the Delaware Bay during the war, often taking large British ships by surprise or stealing them while they were docked. They would then either scuttle, burn, or often hide them in the many small creeks along the shore.

The little seaport of Chestnut Neck, with a population of around 200 folks, had become the transportation hub of the region, from its wharf's mail, supplies, and goods that had been traded for about a decade before the war. When war came, the village expanded its role and soon became the hub of the privateers' shipping and warehousing operations in all of South Jersey. The work of the privateers was no secret, and they openly spoke about their coveted prizes, selling the cargos at public auction and then using the money to support the operations of the privateers. In particular, one event severely upset the British authorities when the patriots captured HMS ships *Venus* and the *Major Pearson* off Sandy Hook. The vessels were towed to Chestnut Neck, off-loaded at the wharf, and the cargos sold; in all they were valued at $500,000 (McMahon, 1973). Both ships were then set on fire and sunk in the river. It is said that the British commander-in-chief in North America, Sir Henry Clinton, vowed to clean out that nest of rebel pirates.

Clinton took action, and in early October 1778, a fleet of nine ships and 300 men arrived and began firing upon the village in the heavy fog of October 6. Now mind you, spies were everywhere at that time, and word had already gotten back to General Washington about the impending attack, so he had sent a force to meet the British; however, they did not arrive in time, and the village, that had also received word, was ready.

It seems that those men who lived in the village always knew this day would come, so men like Micajah Smith, John Mathis, and Joseph Sooy had been provided funds to build an earthen fort at the point and place several cannons to guard against attacks. The good news is the fort was built; the bad news was the few canons that had been placed were unable to be fired in time. However, the battle was still bravely fought by what is figured to be around 200 patriots armed with muskets and whatever else they had to ward off the British attackers. Grossly outmanned and outgunned, the patriots retreated into the woods by nightfall, while the women and children of the village had already left town with their silverware a day before.

Sir Henry Clinton's men landed at the wharf and quickly went about setting fire to the entire village; homes, the Mathis Tavern, storehouses, and even the wharfs were all ablaze by dawn of the 7th. Little was spared and as the army began marching to the Forks and then to Batsto to capture that place as well of course they were repelled by the patriots deep in the woods and soon they fled back to their ships.

Chestnut Neck never returned to its former importance as a Colonial seaport and village. Some of the Patriots returned and rebuilt but most settled just a bit further South and formed the Town of Wrangleboro, known as the City of Port Republic since 1842. It is now a quiet Colonial village in its own right.

During the American Revolution, the "for hire" Patriot Privateers took great pride in their capture of English merchant vessels. In 1778, this advertisement in the Pennsylvania Packet announced that the cargos of ship *Venus* was to be sold off in the village of Chestnut Neck near where she was captured. Ads such as these undoubtedly angered the British commanders and the Loyalists, both of whom were losing the war and their supplies simultaneously.

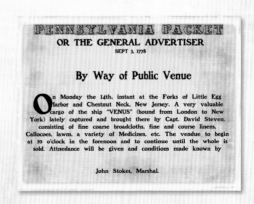

PENNSYLVANIA PACKET
OR THE GENERAL ADVERTISER
SEPT 3, 1778

By Way of Public Venue

On Monday the 14th, instant at the Forks of Little Egg Harbor and Chestnut Neck, New Jersey. A very valuable cargo of the ship "VENUS" (bound from London to New York) lately captured and brought there by Capt. David Steven, consisting of fine coarse broadcloths, fine and course linens, Callocoes, lawns, a variety of Medicines, etc. The vendue to begin at 10 o'clock in the forenoon and to continue until the whole is sold. Attnedance will be given and conditions made known by

John Stokes, Marshal.

Visitor Information

The long-vanished village of Chestnut Neck is reachable by either the Garden State Parkway or US Route 9 in the city (just 1,115 folks) of Port Republic. The village consists of a pull-off along Old New York Road where interpretive signs stand along the battle monument. West of the monument is the burial ground of the Mathis family, which contains around fifteen family members dating back to 1824. The spot is open from dawn to dusk every day; there are no facilities here.

After his original hotel and tavern were destroyed by the British in the 1778 raid, Daniel Mathis rebuilt near the mill pond. Mathis constructed what was later known as the Franklin Inn by 1779 and it was later operated by his son-in-law Jonas Miller. The structure was photographed during a 1935 Historic American Buildings Survey visit and looked to be nearing the end of the road. It was however rebuilt and still stands today, connected to the historic Miller's Store in Port Republic. (The Library of Congress)

The Johnson house, c. 1760, was spared from burning by the British only by the actions of the heart. It has been said that Loyalist James Bell was ordered to burn the place; he soon saw a beautiful young woman, the owner's daughter, Michelle Johnson, run inside. Not intending to murder anyone, he searched for her in vain, but was soon ordered back to the ship, before burning the house. After the war, Bell returned to Chestnut Neck and soon took Miss Johnson's hand in marriage. The beautiful mural of an Atlantic sailing vessel once adorned the east wall of the home's foyer. It remained in remarkable condition despite it having been painted nearly one hundred years prior. The Johnson family continued to live in the home until 1956; these photos were taken in 1960 during an HABS survey. The house and the mural were destroyed by an arson fire in 1965. (The Library of Congress)

Most people in New Jersey have no knowledge of the battle of Chestnut Neck or the massive monument that marks the former town and battle site. In 1911, the monument was erected by the Daughters of the American Revolution and still stands with a proud Chestnut Neck Minuteman perched high above; he seems to be keeping guard just in case the British return on some foggy October morning.

COLONEL RICHARD WESCOAT

Living at The Forks in 1764, he became an ardent patriot and as a First Major, served in Colonel Richard Somers' 3rd Regiment, Gloucester County Militia in 1775. He served at Mt. Holly in a skirmish in Dec. 1776 and was wounded at Trenton Jan. 2, 1777. Wescoat and Elijah Clark constructed the Fort Fox Burrows at Chestnut Neck prior to the battle on Oct. 6, 1778. Moving to Mays Landing in June 1783, he operated a store and tavern close to the present County buildings and died here on Mar. 9, 1825, aged 91 years. He is buried in Presbyterian Cemetery.

HAMILTON TOWNSHIP BI-CENTENNIAL COMMITTEE 1975

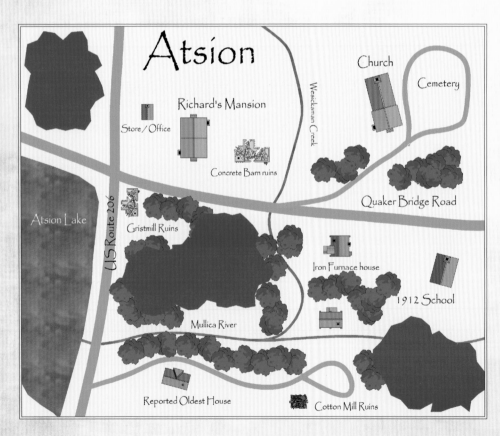

Atsion

Richard's Mansion

Store / Office

Concrete Barn ruins

Wesickaman Creek

Church

Cemetery

Quaker Bridge Road

Atsion Lake

US Route 206

Gristmill Ruins

Mullica River

Iron Furnace house

1912 School

Reported Oldest House

Cotton Mill Ruins

WHARTON STATE FOREST SHAMONG TOWNSHIP, BURLINGTON COUNTY

The early history of Atsion follows closely to the other beginnings of places, like its sister village Batsto and nearby Martha Furnace. Over the first decade, the place changed owners quite frequently. From Charles Read to John Estelle, onto George Marple, James Inskeep, and back to Charles Read. These constant transactions were sure to have kept the county clerk busy in Mount Holly! Read went about enlarging the existing forge and constructed a new furnace along the now dammed Atsion River; workers were kept busy constructing new buildings and keeping the furnace fires smelting the bog iron, which was taken up from nearby lowlands.

By 1819, the isolated village of Atsion floundered; lack of business combined with bad business decisions forced the last residents to leave by 1820. During this time, the houses, furnaces, and other buildings fell into rapid decay. In 1823, Philadelphian John Fanning Watson wrote the following upon riding through the village: "They looked as picturesque as the ruins of abbeys, etc., in pictures. There were dams, forges, furnaces, store-houses, a dozen houses . . . Now all is housed, no wheels turn, no fires ablaze, the houses are unroofed . . . they have fallen down and not a foot of the busy workmen is seen." It appears that Atsion had become the first Jersey ghost town, but it would not be for long.

Samuel Richards purchased the entire Atsion tract in 1824 and set upon putting up a new blast furnace and building, as well as an entirely new village around this iron works. His three and one-half-story Greek revival mansion was completed in 1826. Once home to the grand balls, lavish Christmas mornings, and country life for his family, it still stands today as it was built, having never been modernized.

The famous *Gordon's Gazetteer* of 1834 traversed New Jersey's cities and villages; in it Thomas Gordon wrote:

Atsion, post-town and furnace, on the Atsion River, partly in Galloway Township, Gloucester County, probably in Washington Township, Burlington County, 9 miles above the head of navigation, 12 miles from Medford, 17 from Mount Holly, on the road leading to Tuckerton, and 57 from Trenton. Besides the furnace, there are here, a forge, gristmill, and three sawmills. The furnace makes from 800 to 900 tons of casting, and the forge from 150 to 200 tons of bar iron annually. This estate, belonging to Samuel Richards, Esq., embraces what was formerly called Hampton furnace and forge, and West's Mills, and contains about 60,000 acres of land. There are about 100 men employed here, and between 6 and 700 persons depending for sustenance upon the works.

The village continued to grow and prosper and was known throughout the nation for the construction of the famed Atsion woodstoves, some of which still can be found here and there centuries after they were first cast.

Samuel Richards' fine country Greek revival mansion was completed in 1826, just two years after he arrived in Atsion (pronounced *At-Zine*). It was the focal point of the community and a stopping-off point for weary travelers along the Quaker Bridge Road. It served as the summer home for the Richards. Long abandoned, it was rescued by the state in 1954 and later stabilized and restored. Today, its bright orange-yellow color is uniquely Atsion for all those who pass by on Route 206.

As with Allaire and Batsto, the furnace fires were extinguished for the last time in 1846. Upon the death of Richards, in 1842, the property was divided among his children who, through marriage into the Fleming family of Philadelphia, continued to make changes to Atsion. In 1852, a massive stone and brick paper mill was constructed on the site of the iron furnace; later it was converted into a cotton mill and by 1882, was idled, and Atsion once again became a ghost town.

In later years, Atsion would be renamed Fruitland; then, in 1882, it failed as a master planned city known as Raleigh. Raleigh never came to be a reality, and the name of Atsion returned in the late 1880s, just before the village was absorbed into the expansive Wharton tract along with Harrisville, Batsto, and the other ghost towns of the pines.

A few houses in Atsion remained inhabited by people on and off again for many years while the village store continued to supply items for the farmers in the Atsion area until 1946.

So, little Atsion would have slipped into obscurity had it not been for a few interested souls and the backing of the Batsto Citizens Committee, the group responsible for so much of the saving of that village over the past half-century.

Atsion became a State Recreation Area as part of the Wharton State Forest in mid-1954. Atsion is today a popular swimming area managed by the State Parks while the ancient Quaker Bridge running through Atsion is a favorite jumping off point for those off-road enthusiasts.

The Richards mansion was restored in 2008-09, which was the first major work done to it since it had been stabilized in 1956. It is today open for tours and offers a glimpse into the rural aristocratic life of New Jersey in the mid-nineteenth century. The 1852 paper mill was destroyed in a suspicious 1977 fire, and all that remains today is one large fieldstone chimney. Other buildings that remain include the 1828 church and cemetery, schoolhouse, and a few houses. The village store functions as the park office while the massive concrete barn erected in the 1890s stands roofless next to the mansion.

A visit to Atsion is an interesting trip at any time; winters are especially quiet, and you will often have the place to yourself to explore and enjoy. It remains an outstanding example of another small self-contained community in South Jersey.

Visitor Information

Another of treasure of Wharton State Forest, Atsion Recreation Area, is located along Route 206 in Shamong Township. The village located on the east side of 206 is open from dawn to dusk, 365 days a year. The mansion is open sporadically, and there is no visitor center; however, extensive signage explains much of the history of the village. If you have a four-wheel-drive vehicle, the unmaintained Quaker Bridge Road runs both east and west and takes the capable traveler deep into Wharton, which is an amazing trip into natural New Jersey.

Fire destroyed the original barn at Atsion sometime around 1899. Joseph Wharton, ever mindful of the danger of fire, ensured that his new fireproof poured concrete barn was not going to meet that same fate. Although the barn that housed horses and hay for the farm escaped fire, time has taken its toll on it, and today only the walls remain.

Public School 94 was first built along the old Quaker Bridge Road in 1872. This building was constructed just to the west of the original school in 1912. Many years have gone by since children passed through its doors. Later, having been converted to a private home, it is today in derelict condition.

The small frame building known as the Richards Church or the Free Union Church was most likely constructed sometime around 1825, and has been only slightly changed since that time, Many years ago, its fine arched windows were replaced with square-topped ones, and an addition was added to the main entrance. It has been the Grace Bible Church for many years now.

This one-and-one-half-story dwelling stands just to the west of the old cotton mill site. Believed to be the oldest building in the village, besides the mansion, it may have been built in the 1820s. It was occupied until just a few years ago but now lies empty; however, it is in very good condition—for the time being.

All of the industries that made Atsion prosper are gone: the iron furnace, the railroad, the bogs, and even the cotton mill. Originally built in 1852 as a cotton mill, where after an 1855 fire, it was converted, in 1871, into a paper mill. Later it was used by Joseph Wharton as a cranberry sorting and packing house. Only the main chimney from the mill remains today. It stood until March 27, 1977, when it was destroyed in an arson fire.

Welcome to

FELTVILLE AND SMITHVILLE

Feltville 1736 and 1845

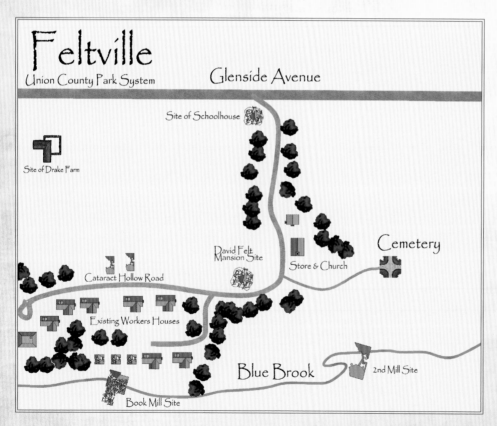

Feltville
Union County Park System

Glenside Avenue

Site of Schoolhouse

Site of Drake Farm

David Felt
Mansion Site

Store & Church

Cemetery

Cataract Hollow Road

Existing Workers Houses

Blue Brook

2nd Mill Site

Book Mill Site

BERKELEY HEIGHTS, UNION COUNTY

One of the first settlers to this area of Union County was an Englishman named Peter Willcox, who came here from Long Island, New York, in 1736. Willcox built a sawmill along the Blue Brook that flourished for a number of years, its location long lost to obscurity. The Willcox family lived and farmed this area for over a century and, by 1800, had established the Willcocks and Badgley Cemetery. This small cemetery has an estimated two dozen burials of family members along with the headstones of three Revolutionary War patriots. John Willcocks, most likely Peter's son, was a member of Captain Marsh's Light Horse Troop, and was killed on November 22, 1776. The cemetery is well marked and maintained today; however, most of the original headstones have disappeared over the centuries.

32

The Willcocks and Badgley Family Cemetery is thought to contain about two dozen graves dating from 1776 to the 1830s. Of those, John Willcocks is interred here; he died from injuries during Washington's retreat from the battle of Fort Lee on November 20, 1776.

In 1844, David Felt purchased the property from Willcox's descendants for the purpose of opening a textile mill and establishing a village that was well hidden away in the Watchung Mountains. Felt named the town, like many others in this book, after himself, and by 1846, the area was known as Feltville. He had completed construction of the three-story mill and associated buildings. He then went about constructing the core of his namesake around a central road known as Cataract Hollow Road, which predates the village by many years.

Here Felt constructed a store with a combination church and school on the second floor, workers houses, and his own house. Although history has been kind to Felt, his moniker was King Felt, named by his villagers. He was known as a very strict and demanding owner and manager. When 1850 arrived, nearly 200 people were living and working in Feltville, producing books and other bound articles in the large mill.

Felt retired in 1860, putting an end to the paper binding mill, named Stationers Hall Press. The property passed through a good number of hands for the next twenty years. During that time, many residents left for work elsewhere, and Feltville became a ghost town for the first time in its life in the late 1870s. As with other locales in this book, a company town was dependent upon its industry and the economy; these two fragile links often failed, thereby creating the Jersey ghost towns that we know today.

By 1882, the American people began to find time for recreation in New Jersey; places like Lake Hopatcong, Long Branch, and Cape May began to cater to the now well known summer tourist season. It was at this time that a gentleman named Warren Ackerman, purchased Feltville and changed its name to Glenside Park, where he quickly went about creating a first-class recreation facility. Centered around a bathing lake and summer rental cottages that Ackerman transformed from the old workers homes, Glenside Park achieved a fairly popular following for over three decades but fell out of the times during World War I.

In 1927, the newly formed Union County Park Commission purchased the property as part of the Watchung Reservation. The Commission then allowed persons displaced in the Great Depression to live in the houses and take care of the village, a move which surely saved most of the place from definite ruin. A common but not very fact-based legend of the place is that, in 1912, three young sisters all vanished from their home during a walk in the woods. By the next day, only their bonnets were found, and most of the folks left town in a hurry. Of those who remained, children were no longer allowed into the woods.

Most of the buildings in the village continued to be occupied until about 1970; after that only a handful of residents have remained in this unique place.

Visitor Information

Arriving at Feltville today is pretty easy, located just off Route 78 on Glenside Avenue (where did that name ever come from?); the Park Commission has a well signed parking area established. It will be a little bit of a walk down Cataract Hollow Road, but when you arrive you will first see the store and church, which is covered with rustic stick porches and railings, a renovation from the Glenside Park Area, and during a time rustification was popular in parks throughout the nation. Ongoing restoration efforts are obvious and this place remains a charming slice of another industrious company village in New Jersey.

This photographic transition shows one of the larger workers' homes at Feltville when occupied. The village homes were rusticated during their use as a summer resort, although the homes retained their simple industrial architecture of the 1850s.

Feltville's combined company store and unique second-floor church were constructed between 1845 and 1847. David Felt required all of his employees to attend Sunday church services in the old building. The building was home to the US Post Office starting in 1851 and today serves the Union County Park Commission as a small museum, where restrooms and an ice-cold water fountain are to be found out back, a surely needed treat on a ninety-degree August day!

Like Allaire, Feltville had been known as the Deserted Village, even though it was only truly deserted for a short period of time. Her streets have been home to many over the years, and in the twenty-first century folks still call Feltville home—mostly all employees of the Union County Park Commission.

Many of the workers' houses in the village were completed between 1845 and 1850. The dormers and porches were added later during the Glenside Park years. The rear of this house retains the simple, no nonsense construction that Felt embraced for their design. Of course, this small house is a double house—remember, living in a 400 square-foot home with three children was not commonplace in 1850!

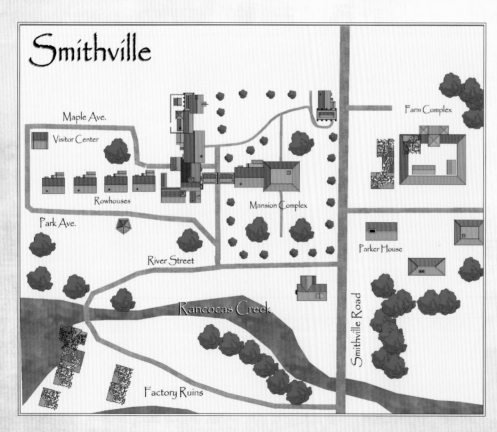

Smithville

Maple Ave.

Visitor Center

Rowhouses

Park Ave.

River Street

Rancocas Creek

Factory Ruins

Farm Complex

Mansion Complex

Parker House

Smithville Road

EASTAMPTON TOWNSHIP, BURLINGTON COUNTY

Burlington County's historic Smithville Park was once the site of several successful endeavors, most notably the H. B. Smith Machinery Works which flourished from 1865 until nearly a century later. Located just a few short miles east of Mount Holly, the spot was first a small mill village begun by Jacob Parker about 1776. The mills prospered until the arrival of the Shreve brothers in 1831. Shreveville was first established in 1831, by brothers Jonathan and Samuel Shreve as a textile factory town on the banks of the Rancocas Creek. The two constructed several new mills and also made use of a variety of existing buildings already on site. The year 1840 saw the erection of a grand Greek revival mansion with elaborately landscaped lawns. Aside from the magnificent mansion, the brothers also constructed two streets of houses. On Maple Avenue, the entire street was lined with three-story brick townhouses, which all stood until about 1950, giving the place the look and feel of aristocratic Philadelphia of the time. The factory flourished and many Burlington County men found work there even after the site was purchased by Hezekiah Bradley Smith in 1865. Smith went about expanding the village and soon renamed the place Smithville, where the US post office was commissioned in 1866.

Throughout our country in the mid nineteenth century factory towns were at their zenith. For the owners of these places having your workers on site was beneficial: you could control most aspects of their lives, which were more or less devoted to the operation that the owner conducted. For many of these towns—Batsto, Allaire, and others—moving out was nearly impossible as cash was not paid, only company script to be used at the company store. Everything that you required for life was there and there you would stay, sometimes for generations.

But Smithville wasn't just another company town, it was a model company town, said to have been far ahead of its time with the way its 400 workers were treated. First-class housing, a town band, a

Hezekiah Bradley Smith was born on July 24, 1816, in Bridgewater, Vermont. Smith arrived in Shreveville in 1865, quickly changing the place to Smithville. An incredible inventor and machinist, he may have built the first automobile powered by kerosene in 1879. His life is an interesting tale of inventions, patents, politics, two wives (at the same time), angry children, and success.

bowling alley, generous time off, and clean working conditions, along with good wages all existed under the ownership of Hezekiah Smith. Smith built the massive Mechanic's Hall in 1870, part dormitory, mess hall for his employees, and most notably an 800-seat opera house.

Starting in 1880, the Smith factories began turning out the first High Wheel bicycles of the American Star Patent. These fragile bicycles were all the craze of the later part of the nineteenth century and were eventually replaced by the much safer and stable style of bicycle we know today.

In 1892, the Smith Company received an unusual order, to engineer and construct a nearly two-mile-long bicycle railroad from Mount Holly to Smithville. The bicycle railway consisted of a monorail-type design where the rider could pedal without steering, and very fast speeds could be obtained, possibly leading to the famous moniker: Look ma', no hands. The railroad was utilized for just seven short years; however, the industrious design lives on in many transportation ideas to this day.

The Smith factories were often visited by folks from around the world to marvel at the ingenious operations of the machine shops, where by 1880, he was producing a quarter of all woodworking machines in the nation. One point of interest was the 110-foot-tall observation tower that Smith constructed in 1878, allowing a good view over most of Burlington, Monmouth, and Ocean Counties on a clear day.

The H. B. Smith Company continued to operate after Smith's death in 1887, operated by his son until c. 1930. The Great Depression put an end to the factories that had been busy for nearly a century. In 1962, the property finally passed out of the Smith family and, in 1975, became the first unit of the Burlington County Park System.

Over the last forty years, the county has not only preserved but restored many of the buildings at the site, making this one of the finest of our Jersey ghost towns. It remains the largest and most prominent of all the lost villages in New Jersey.

Visitor Information

Burlington County's Park System centerpiece is the Historic Smithville Park and Smith's Woods. Located at 803 Smithville Road, in Eastampton Twp (Mount Holly mailing address), the place is not far from the NJ Turnpike or Burlington County 537. The park is open daily from dawn to dusk and has a newly renovated visitor center (609-265-5858) and comfort station located near the main parking lot. The Smith Mansion is open for tours on an irregular basis, so be sure to call, because a tour of the mansion is well worth the trip. Smith's Woods offers picnic areas and restrooms as well.

Smithville's elegant Greek revival mansion was finished in 1840, originally occupied by the Shreve Brothers, Jonathan and Samuel, the founders of Shreveville. When Hezekiah Smith arrived in 1865, he went about expanding not just the village but the mansion as well. Smith lived here with his wife, Agnes, until his death in 1887; it has been meticulously restored.

The famed American Star bicycle was invented by George W. Pressey of Hammonton in 1888. The H. B. Smith became the manufacturer for these oddities that became all the craze of the Gay '90s. They were seen as so innovative that one remains on display in the transportation exhibit of the Smithsonian Institution in Washington, DC.

The Parker-Wright house is the oldest structure not only in the village but in all of Eastampton Township as well. Probably built in 1750, it was the second of two houses constructed for the owner of the grist mill along the Rancocas Creek. It is typical of mid-eighteenth century West Jersey farmhouses found throughout the region from Delaware to Pennsylvania.

One of the oldest houses in the village was built as this 1831 workers' cottage from the Shreveville time period and still stands, nearly 200 years after its construction. Recently the county restored the building and combined a modern visitor center and comfort station into the structure. Burlington's Park System has slowly been returning the town to its 1870s appearance since it acquired the property in 1975.

Smith organized a well-trained volunteer fire department for his village, consisting of his employees. Fire hydrants were placed throughout the place to ensure rapid connections to be made just in case a blaze broke out. It was reported that ample water pressure was available from the large water tank. They must have been an efficient department as there is no record of major fires in the early years of its operation.

Upon arriving in the village, Smith tore down nearly all of the existing small brick workers' cottages and built these much larger frame dwellings on their foundations. They all remain today and most have been restored, standing on Park Avenue overlooking the band gazebo and the mill pond. Smith built an incredibly modern, upscale community in a rather desolate location that thrived and prospered due to his modern philosophies on management and people.

Smith constructed a large variety of woodworking and cabinet building machinery. Planers, joiners, lathes, and saws were all turned out of his busy factory. He employed over 150 persons in the machinery business and was able to receive patents for over forty different machines during his lifetime.

Welcome to
DOUBLE TROUBLE AND WHITESBOG

Double Trouble
Drouble Trouble State Park

1. School 1893
2. Burke House 190
3. Blacksmith Shop / Garage
4. Cranberry Packing House
5. General Store   1920
6. Shower Room
7. Bunk House 1900
8. Cook House Site
9. Pickers Cottage
10. Jumper Building
11. Sawmill
12. Foremans House 190
13. Pickers Cottage
14. Pickers Cottage
15. Foremans House

Park entrance from Pinewald-Keswick road

DOUBLE TROUBLE STATE PARK BERKELEY TOWNSHIP, OCEAN COUNTY
c. 1860

Crane-berries you say, what in the world is a crane-berry? Well, once upon a time, that is exactly what today's cranberries were first called by our early settlers, named for their crooked stem that resembles a crane's neck. South Jersey is the king of cranberry farming in the northeast and, according the State of New Jersey, ranks third in production of this delicious berry. Out in Ocean County, the Double Trouble Company got its start in 1903 when Edward Crabbe changed the place over from sawmill town to a private cranberry company, which soon became one of the largest growers of cranberries in the state as his cranmeadows soon covered hundreds of acres.

In every cranberry harvesting operation the sorting and packing house was most critical to the farm's prosperity. Double Trouble's was completed in 1909 with a host of additions through 1925. The once-busy building was restored in 1996 and is today open at times for tours. (The Library of Congress)

The tiny Double Trouble schoolhouse was originally part of the incorporated village of Double Trouble dating to 1893. When the village became a self-supporting cranberry farm, the school continued to be used for the employee's children until 1915. Its unusual architecture is uncommon to nineteenth-century one-room schools.

Within a few years, the rather isolated Double Trouble farm had taken over the old lumber mill town. Crabbe kept the name Double Trouble, which is said to have been named after two earthen dams broke in quick succession and the manager of the mill exclaimed, "That's Double Trouble!". In no time at all, new buildings sprung up to support the operation, such as the packing and sorting house, along with pickers cottages and the village staple for village staples, the General Store.

Double Trouble operated as a private farm for over one hundred years until the property was purchased by the State of New Jersey in 1964. However, even as the old village became state property, the cranberry harvests did not stop, as the Crabbe family continued to plant until 1970.

Farming of the bogs continued until 2011, and since then none of the little red bouncing berries have been grown at Double Trouble; hopefully they will return soon.

Visitor Information

When you get to Double Trouble State Park you can find the entrance on Pinewald-Keswick Road/Ocean County 618. A short drive down a pine needle-covered sand road and you will quickly arrive in the village. Some of the buildings, including the packing house are restored and open for tours, bathrooms are located here, but there are no other facilities. In all, Double Trouble State Park consists of just under 8,500 acres with the village area taking up 200 acres. It is a nice mix of restored and original buildings, and a few that need more than a little TLC; however, it is still a working farm—the old place just needs a good cranberry farmer.

Typical of the many general stores that dotted rural New Jersey from the 1830s to the 1960s, the Double Trouble store was built in 1920. It was the heart of the village life and the place where good news was celebrated and bad news was mulled over. It continued to operate until the village was sold to the state in 1964.

One of the relics on display outside the sorting and packing house is this horse-drawn road grader. In the days of unpaved roads, the road grader was an incredibly important machine to remove wagon ruts, crown roads for better drainage, and even plow winter snows to keep the roads open.

This photo captures the employees of Double Trouble loading empty cranberry crates onto a 1936 Chevy Stake body truck. The busy season for the cranberry farmers meant employing a seasonal workforce, local day laborers, and even families looking to make some extra cash. It was tough, hot work, and the use of machinery has made it a little easier over the years.

Another finely preserved building at Double Trouble is this manager's house. Due to the remote location of the town, it was required that most of the management of the cranberry pickers live on site. The accommodations were by no means lavish; however, they were warm, dry, and allowed family members to stay with the all male supervisory staff during the operation of Double Trouble.

The Foreman of the Double Trouble Company lived in this small-frame one-story house near the village school. One of the few year-round employees, the Foreman supervised the cranberry farm as well as the sawmill operation. This house was built in 1900.

This 1991 photograph was taken as part of the HABS and captures the unrestored sawmill in derelict condition. This building is the largest structure in the village and contains most of the original machinery still intact. The first sawmill here was completed in 1765 along the Cedar Creek; this structure was restored in 1995. (The Library of Congress)

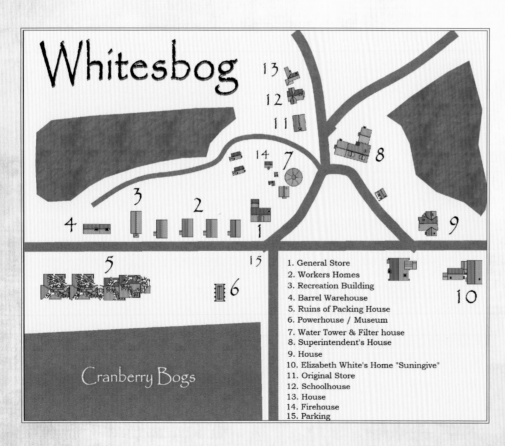

Whitesbog

1. General Store
2. Workers Homes
3. Recreation Building
4. Barrel Warehouse
5. Ruins of Packing House
6. Powerhouse / Museum
7. Water Tower & Filter house
8. Superintendent's House
9. House
10. Elizabeth White's Home "Suningive"
11. Original Store
12. Schoolhouse
13. House
14. Firehouse
15. Parking

Cranberry Bogs

BRENDAN T. BYRNE STATE FOREST PEMBERTON TOWNSHIP, BURLINGTON COUNTY

The future village known as Whitesbog can trace its early beginnings to the cranberry farm that Colonel James Fenwick established in the early 1850s on about 490 acres in central Burlington County. It was near the colonial site of the famed Hanover Furnace that Fenwick was able to successfully cultivate his cranberry crops, which eventually led to the cranberry industry taking off like wildfire throughout South Jersey.

Although Fenwick was a well-established and respected cranberry farmer in the area, it was his daughter's marriage to another cranberry farmer in 1869, that truly grew the company into the king of New Jersey cranberry producers. Josiah J. White, better known as J. J., married Mary Fenwick and they were soon operating their bogs as a separate and very successful operation farm not far from Fenwick's property. In 1882, Col. Fenwick died, leaving his farms to the Whites, who went on managing Fenwick's bogs until the death of Mrs. Fenwick in 1912. It was during this year that the J. J. White Company was established, and Whitesbog became a place on the map after that.

Employing modern techniques and plenty of farmhands, Whitesbog became the center of New Jersey cranberry production, and the village itself was laid out along several streets among the sandy Main Street and towering pines. Comfortable seasonal workers' houses were finished along with a large general store, which was nestled under the town's water tower. Of all the communities in this book, only Whitesbog provided their own water system and did not rely solely on wells for domestic water and fire protection, a testament of J. J.'s commitment to owning and managing a modern company town. The massive cranberry packing and sorting warehouse was built in 1890 and added on to in 1900. This building was only second to the bogs themselves; here dozens of workers sorted the good and bad berries, cleaned them, and packed them into barrels to be shipped around the nation. The work was hard, the pay said to be fair, but complaints happened, and for those who lived and worked in Whitesbog, most everyone earned a good living.

Not only was Whitesbog the cranberry capital of New Jersey, it soon became known for its blueberry crops as well. J. J.'s daughter, Elizabeth, spent her life—from 1893 on—working and living in the village, where she was known for cultivating the first successful blueberry bush in the world.

Elizabeth lived her entire life in the house that she had built in 1923, known as Suningive, which still stands next to her world-renowned gardens. These gardens contain many of her plantings from just before her death in 1954 and remain in excellent condition.

Known as the Blueberry Queen, Elizabeth was a tireless advocate for workers rights and good living conditions and, along with her father, assisted the state in the creation of the New Lisbon Developmental Center for children.

Eatmor Cranberries was the trade name of the National Fruit Exchange, comprised of growers from several states. This label, dating from about 1920, was given to the J. R. Brick Company of Medford. J. R. Brick and family are still active growers in Burlington County and sort and pack their brand in a 200-year old barn in Medford Village.

Whitesbog is today part of Brendan T. Byrne State Forest, where 37,000 acres of pine forest, cranberry bogs, and blueberry bushes make up the state's second largest natural area.

The Whitesbog Preservation Trust is a nonprofit organization that has managed the restoration of the village for several decades. The village tract and bogs make up about 3,000 acres, along with many restored buildings and a few private residences that are leased from the state.

Most of the buildings from the village's heyday remain; however, the packing and sorting house was destroyed by two separate fires in the 1960s and 1980s; ironically only the firewalls remain.

The village's focal point today is the Whitesbog General Store, normally open on weekends throughout the year; check out *www.whitesbog.org* for the most current information. If in the area, be sure to check out the heavily visited Whitesbog Blueberry Festival held each June for the past three decades; it is a slice of Pinelands life that you don't want to miss.

Visitor Information

Whitesbog Village is located on Whitesbog Road directly off Lakehurst Road (Burlington CR 530).

Construction of the Whitesbog Sorting and Packing House was completed in three stages between 1890 and 1905. This building contained nearly 25,000 square feet of working space among two spacious floors that also included an indoor railroad track for moving the heavy berries. For nearly seventy years the building was the recipient of millions of delicious cranberries that were harvested each autumn. It was destroyed by two fires in 1961 and 1970; it today lies in ruins. (The Library of Congress)

The store has remained unchanged since the prior photo was taken for the HABS in 1989. It still operated as a busy store by the Whitesbog Trust and carries an assortment of Pine Barrens products, including local honey and both cranberry and blueberry preserves. Nearly thirty years after this photo was taken, the same soda machine is still out front!

Whitesbog's first general store was opened for business in 1899 and stood in this spot under the water tower until 1923. After a post office was commissioned in 1923, the old store was moved and replaced by this structure in 1924. The old store became a home after it was moved and still stands. (The Library of Congress)

The barrel factory was built in March of 1907 where coopers constructed the wooden barrels that the cranberries were packed in before shipping. With advances in shipping containers, barrels were abandoned in 1925 for wooden boxes. At this time J. J. White transformed the factory into a community center and recreation hall for his employees and residents.

The wooden water tower overlooks eighty-four feet of the village and holds nearly 30,000 gallons of water. Both the town's drinking water and fire protection came from this gravity tank, which was constructed of iron-banded wood in 1914. It was restored in the early 1990s. Beside the local Lebanon Fire Tower, it is one of the tallest structures in the area.

Suningive was the name of Elizabeth White's lifelong adult home in Whitesbog. Elizabeth had the cedar shingle residence constructed with plans that the first floor would be used as the company office, a function it never fulfilled. Elizabeth lived in the home and worked on her famous blueberry cultivation science from there. It is today the office for the Whitesbog Preservation Trust. (The Library of Congress)

The row of houses between the community center and the general store were all built in 1895. Originally housing four families each in very cramped quarters, they had no running water or electricity. They were later converted into year-round two-family homes. Italian immigrants from Philadelphia comprised much of the seasonal workforce, and though the work was tough, a good wage could be earned to support their families during the off season.

The barrel warehouse was constructed in time for the 1911 fall harvest season. It is made up of sixteen separate partitions, each with an exterior sliding door for access. Not only did it provide storage for barrels but was used as an overflow packing house when the main building was out of room. It is one of the few painted buildings in the village and has a very festive feel to it with its white board and batten siding, green-trimmed doors, and red metal seamed roof.

Whitesbog's one-room school was used for just ten short years starting in 1908. The school was attached to the school teacher's home. After it was closed in 1918, village children attended school in Pemberton Township. It has since been restored.

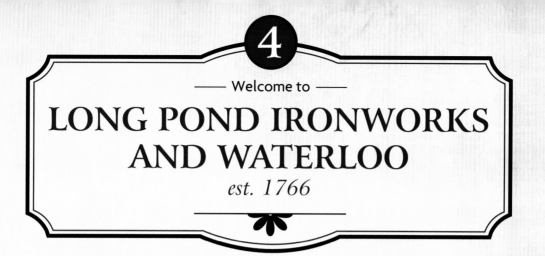

WEST MILFORD TOWNSHIP, PASSAIC COUNTY

Long Pond Ironworks was one of a string of important ironworks that existed prior, during, and after the American Revolution in North Jersey, then known as East Jersey. In 1766, German-born ironmaster Peter Hasenclever purchased the property, which also contained the already operating Ringwood Ironworks, begun in 1742.

Hasenclever built the Long Pond and Charlottenburg Iron works, along with 55,000 acres comprising much of Passaic and Bergen Counties. These vast land holdings were the creation of a complex ironworks, farming, and industrial area, where more than 500 German immigrants were brought in to work and live in the area. By the dawn of the Revolution, Robert Erskine replaced Hasenclever as manager at Long Pond,

Legend

1. Visitor Center / Former Store
2. House
3. Laird-West House
4. Ward-Ryerson-Paterson House
5. Whritenour House
6. Milligan - Harty House
7. Barn
8. Stone House
9. Manager's House
10. Village Store Ruins
11. Icehouse Ruins
12. Blacksmith Shop Site
13. Revolutionary Iron Furnace
14. Waterwheel Ruins
15. Civil War Iron Furnace Ruins
16. Hewitt Church
17. House
18. House

Long Pond Ironworks
West Milford, NJ

Greenwood Lake Road

and during the war, the furnace supplied invaluable munitions, shot, and iron supplies for Washington's Army. Robert Erskine died at Ringwood on October 2, 1780, and was buried in the village cemetery. It is of interest to note that Long Pond is actually the Native American name for Greenwood Lake, the actual body of water that is located here.

During the first part of the nineteenth century, the ironworks changed hands twice and, in 1853, was bought by Peter Cooper and Abram S. Hewitt, who enlarged the works and built two new furnace stacks between 1861 and 1865. Both men were already successful ironworks owners and had been operating the Trenton ironworks in Mercer County since 1847. Long Pond, by then taking the name of Hewitt, began producing the refined iron for making gun barrels for the Union Army. By 1870, Hewitt and the Ironworks were home to several hundred workers. To get an idea of how large this area was, Ringwood Manor, which was the home of the owners of Long Pond, is nearly five miles from the center of the Village.

Long Pond's demise was the same as the rest of the iron towns; with the founding of iron ore in the Pennsylvania Mountains, one by one the New Jersey furnaces closed. Long Pond's furnace fires were put out forever in 1882; however, other industries continued -- mining

as well as ice cutting were major contributors to the area's economy for many years to come.

In 1895, a new church was constructed, and a new saw mill opened for business in 1905. Hewitt continued as a typical village with a small population supporting ice cutting and storage, as well as mining, which still exists today. In 1937, Ringwood Manor was donated to the state by the Hewitt family, and by 1957, Long Pond ironworks was also donated. The Village of Hewitt, however, did not vanish. It simply migrated up the road a piece and still is a village within West Milford Township.

Visitor Information

A visit to Long Pond Ironworks today will take you to the Long Pond Ironworks State Park; at just about 7,000 acres, it is one of the largest parks in the Garden State. The Ironworks Visitor Center opened in 1996 in the former village store and is operated by the Friends of Long Pond Ironworks, Inc. Current information is available from longpondironworks. org. All of the village sites, including the 1766 Iron Furnace and both Civil War-era furnaces, can be seen along with a collection of homes and utilitarian buildings that were built from colonial times throughout the 1890s. It is a good hike through the village and is one of the more spread-out villages in this book. Other than the Visitor Center and Museum there are no other facilities at the site, so pack what you need and bring bug spray, please. After visiting the site, a side trip to Ringwood Manor nicely ties the five centuries of the ironworks together.

Long Pond is reached by Passaic County Route 511, locally known as the Greenwood Lake Turnpike in Hewitt, NJ.

Famed American Industrialist Abram S. Hewitt was born in Haverstraw, New York, in 1822. He became business partners with the famed New York City figure Peter Cooper and eventually his son-in-law in 1855. Two years prior to this, Hewitt and Cooper had purchased the Long Pond Ironworks and the adjoining forests. Cooper was a railroad developer, shipwreck survivor, and known as a philanthropist to many during his life. He and Cooper modernized Long Pond, and within a few years, the entire community became known as Hewitt, a name it still bears along with the State Forest that was named in his honor. (The Library of Congress)

Though not original to the village limits, it is believed that the Ward-Ryerson-Paterson House could have been built as early as 1775. Renovated and changed to fit the architectural trends of the times, it eventually became a restaurant known as the Wanaque Valley Inn in the 1930s. It remained in that incarnation until about 1980 when it was moved to escape the rising waters of the Monksville Reservoir. It was placed on a new foundation in the village and has sat idle since. It is a nice example of the Hudson Valley Dutch colonial style and is similar to the Van Horn House in Mahwah. (The Library of Congress)

The Stites house is another structure that is original to the village. Constructed about 1860, it is of simple architecture consistent with buildings built throughout the state for company employees. The boarded-up windows were painted to resemble windows, a common method in disguising vacant buildings used at Allaire during the early years of restoration.

THE LONG POND IRONWORKS
HISTORIC VILLAGE OF HEWITT

Founded in 1766 by Peter Hasenclever, the Long Pond Ironworks was run by a succession of famous ironmasters, including Robert Erskine, Martin J. Ryerson and Abram S. Hewitt. The Long Pond furnace, forge and supporting village contributed to the war efforts during the American Revolution, the War of 1812 and the Civil War. As at many other iron-producing sites in the Highlands, the furnace operation at Long Pond ended in the 1880s when the iron industry's western migration was complete.

Long Pond was the colonial name for Greenwood Lake, the source of waterpower for the 18th- and 19th-century iron-smelting complex.

The Long Pond Ironworks Historic District is listed on the State and National Registers of Historic Places.

ERECTED BY THE FRIENDS OF LONG POND IRONWORKS,
THE NORTH JERSEY DISTRICT WATER SUPPLY COMMISSION
AND THE HACKENSACK WATER CO.

51

The remains of the ice house near the crumbling Village Store make for a medieval feel deep in the woods. Both buildings face Furnace Road and were built in 1760 and rebuilt a century later. The stone company store existed until the 1920s, when the operation moved to the new company store, which is today the visitor center and museum.

The third generation of iron furnace construction was completed under the management of Cooper and Hewitt. It was in 1860 that this furnace was completed to ensure production throughout the Civil War years. It may be the last charcoal blast furnace constructed in New Jersey. It is today a ruin of sandstone blocks and Gothic arches deep in the Abram S. Hewitt State Forest.

Long Pond's Milligan-Harty home was constructed just prior to the Civil War as a double house for the employees of the iron works. It is stone construction with a coating of stucco on the exterior and was rebuilt in the 1990s; it is in relatively good condition.

Hewitt's Methodist congregation completed this frame house of worship in 1895. Although the blast furnace had been extinguished in 1882, the community did not die. There was still work to be done, and those folks soon found other livelihoods keeping the village alive. The church remains in good condition but is not actively used.

The grand country estate home known as Ringwood Manor was begun in 1807 by Martin Ryerson. The ten-room house was set upon over 11,000 acres, which comprised both the Ringwood and Long Pond Ironworks operations. In 1853, Cooper and Hewitt purchased all of this property and inherited Ringwood as their summer home. The Hewitt family lived and loved the place dearly, adding onto it in 1864, 1875, 1900, and 1910. When finished, Ringwood Manor boasted fifty-one rooms and was one of the largest homes in New Jersey. In 1938, the Hewitt family donated the home and property to the State of New Jersey to form the nucleus of two parks: Ringwood Manor State Park and Abram S. Hewitt State Forest. (The Library of Congress)

— Welcome to —
WATERLOO
est. 1760

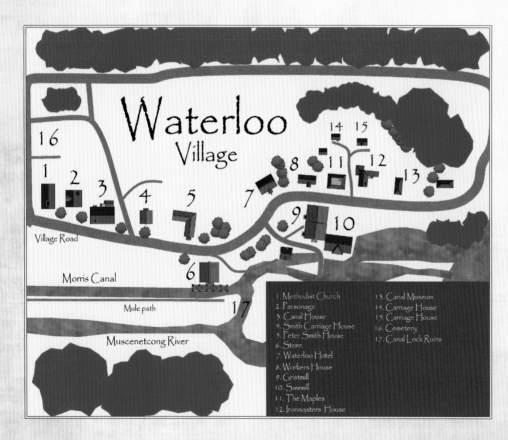

Waterloo Village

Village Road

Morris Canal

Mule path

Muscenetcong River

16
1 2 3 4 5 7 8 11 12 13 14 15 9 10 17 6

1. Methodist Church
2. Parsonage
3. Canal House
4. Smith Carriage House
5. Peter Smith House
6. Store
7. Waterloo Hotel
8. Workers House
9. Gristmill
10. Sawmill
11. The Maples
12. Ironmasters House
13. Canal Museum
14. Carriage House
15. Carriage House
16. Cemetery
17. Canal Lock Ruins

ALLAMUCHY STATE PARK STANHOPE, SUSSEX COUNTY

The history of Waterloo Village is one of the most complex of all the towns visited in this book. Dating back to 1760 and having several distinct purposes for the village, it is today a mix of colonial, nineteenth century industrial, and Victorian architecture. As with all villages, the buildings are only part of the story, but are the one constant that remains to tell of the people and events that shaped our nation.

It was along the banks of the Musconetcong River that the first iron forge was built here in 1761, then known as Andover Forge. It operated throughout the Revolution, and during this time, many new buildings were completed. By 1780, there was the iron forge, charcoal house, gristmill, sawmill, blacksmith shop, and three stone dwellings.

Remember that this area was adjacent to the vast wilderness of this time, and this operation was extremely remote from other places—it was nearly a thirty-mile journey to Morristown alone. The remoteness of the place surely contributed to its eventual sale and constant changing of hands in the last decade of the eighteenth century. The year 1795 saw the forge retired, and the site was closed down for good ending a short run of thirty-five years of iron operations.

The gristmill was kept in operation for the local farmers and their needs, but no other trades were carried on at the time. Like other towns we have looked at, the place waned and became a ghost town for several decades. In fact, had it not been for the completion of the engineering marvel of the Morris Canal, Waterloo would be only a blurb in history books and the rubble of collapsed buildings. The Morris Canal arrived at the yet-to-be-named village site in 1831, and it had been envisioned by the new owner, John Smith, that the old forge property would be the perfect place to create a transportation hub where canal, roads, and rail could all someday meet.

During this time, Smith renovated all of the long decrepit forge buildings, relocating and giving them new life. The canal was now in operation while those mule-powered canal boats were a daily sight passing through the locks of the village. In 1830, Smith constructed the three-and-one-half-story general store, and it was this store that became the soul of the village for decades serving as the loading and unloading point for the canal boats in the back doors and the transfer of merchandise and supplies out the front doors to the people. Smith saw his vision fulfilled when the Morris and Essex Railroad put their standard gauge tracks through the village in 1855.

New buildings were completed throughout the 1830s and 1870s; this period of prosperity was fueled by the Civil War and the massive amount of supplies and goods that traveled through the Morris Canal to support the Union. After the 1870s, the second generation of Smiths took the reins of the village, and business at Waterloo slowed a bit over the next twenty years; however, new Victorian homes were built by family members—remember the Smiths were wealthy before Waterloo; the canal and village only made them wealthier over the years. The village continued on, but by the turn of the next century, dark days were looming. In 1902, the railroad, now owned by the

Village Store and Post Office, A. L. Cassedy, Waterloo, N. J.

Waterloo's General Store was completed along the banks of the Morris Canal in 1831. Built of native Jersey fieldstone, the three-story structure formed the nucleus of the village's trade. The black and white photo was taken about 1899, and the color photo in 2011. The State Forest Fire Service, Division A, utilized it as their headquarters during the Great Depression. It remains an outstanding example of New Jersey's transportation heritage and the importance of the once mighty Morris Canal. (The Library of Congress)

Delaware Lackawanna and Western, moved the mainline away from Waterloo to Stanhope. Twelve months later, the last Morris Canal officially closed (though no boats had used it much since the 1880s).

By 1910, the village was mostly occupied by tenants of the Smith family, who continued to own Waterloo; in the 1920s, the family had

The true business end of the Smith Store was the side that faced the canal. The loading and unloading of goods and supplies from the canal boats among the shouts of the boat captains and lock tenders surely made for a lively scene in the village's heyday. The store functioned as the post office as well from 1847 until the demise of the village in the 1930s. (The Library of Congress)

created a development company to subdivide the entire village, a plan that was thwarted by the Great Depression, although the model home that was built still remains.

After more than a century, the economy had crushed the Smiths's remaining wealth and the property was foreclosed on. Waterloo was empty again; the grand balls and parties on the mansion lawns were silent as were the village stores.

It has been told time and again that the place would have fallen into ruin had it not been for those sometimes ragged folks who traveled the rails searching for work or just plain escaping life: the hobo. My own maternal grandfather, Harry Myers, train hobo, most likely passed through Waterloo after skipping out on his family in Johnson City, New York, in 1935. It was these hobos who found Waterloo a kind of stopping-off point from riding the rails: Here they could get shelter, cook, socialize, imbibe in those intoxicating liquors, and do whatever hobos did then.

The side effect of the hobos making Waterloo their home is that they kept it from burning down or falling down or both. The village survived better than Harry Myers, who fell off a train the next year and was instantly killed.

By 1962, two historic minded men, Percy Leach, who had been raised in the village, and his partner, Louis Gualand, began acquiring the entire village piece by piece. By 1964, they had opened some of the restored buildings to the public as a private park. Just as the Tocks Island Dam project nearly wiped out Walpack and her sister towns, the Army Corps of Engineers had planned a dam along the Musconetcong in response to the same 1955 hurricane flooding aftermaths. This plan was finally defeated but not until the state had acquired about fifty percent of the other half of Waterloo village that Percy and Louis had not purchased.

By 1976, the Waterloo Foundation for the Arts had been formed and would operate as the leasee for the entire village property for thirty mostly successful years. Over the years, Waterloo flourished as an arts and public music venue location. Ultimately, the village failed after getting too big for its britches, and by 2006, all state funding for Waterloo dried up. So the village became stuck in a state of suspended animation. Thankfully, within the last few years a new leasing partner has been found, and it is hopeful that some of the buildings can be restored or stabilized.

Visitor Information

Visiting Waterloo today is at least a half-day trip if you are moving quickly. There is much to see, and for someone who loves our New Jersey history, so much of it was made here in Waterloo. I would highly recommend John R. Giles', recent publication, *The Story of Waterloo Village, From Colonial Forge to Canal Town* for an incredible in-depth history of the people and places of Waterloo. Today's Waterloo Village is part of Allamuchy Mountain State Park, located at 525 Waterloo Road in Byram Township just off Interstate 80.

As the importance of the canal began to be realized, additional workmen and their families took up residence in the village. In 1840, this stone two-family house was completed on the same hill that the church stands upon. It is a unique version of a Delaware Valley Greek revival dwelling with frieze band windows and symmetrical lines used in its design.

After the village outgrew worshipping in the old school, the Smith family built this frame house of worship in 1859–1860 on a knoll overlooking the main street of the town. Utilized by the Methodist congregation since that time, they established a cemetery in 1860 that is still in use. Throughout the ups and downs of Waterloo, the church has always been used and well maintained.

This street view is looking toward the white stuccoed Waterloo Hotel. Among the oldest building in this village, it was part of original Andover Forge and built about 1760. Used as both a private dwelling and an inn during its life, it was nearly converted into a convalescent home in 1963. The purchase and subsequent restoration of this building by Percy Leach and Lou Gualandi marked the beginning of the town's restoration.

Another of the original village buildings is this house dating from 1760. Over the centuries it has been remodeled several times and expanded. Peter Smith, the founder of Waterloo Village proper, made this his home for his adult life. It also received stucco over stone treatment in later years and is one of several imposing homes in the village.

The intricate canal lock system was crucial in allowing boats to change the grade of bodies of water. This photo captures the remains of Waterloo Lock as it exists today. The engineering behind the canal lock system dates back to 1200 AD in China and has changed little since that time. Without the slow operation of the lock, canal boats would have floated through Waterloo without stopping; the lock caused a stoppage, and a town was born for America's first rest stop.

Waterloo's gristmill was constructed in 1760 as the Charcoal House for the Andover Forge. Later, when Waterloo was resurrected, Peter Smith rebuilt the building turning it into a mill. Powered by a sluiceway from the Musconetcong River, the water-powered grindstones did the work just as they did in Batsto and other mills across the country. It was restored long ago and is in good condition today.

Right: Standing watch over the village since 1871, this stately Second Empire beauty is known as the Maples. Home to the Smith family from its construction until 1918, the house has weathered a few storms in her day. Typical adornments of the Second Empire style on the Maples include the large curved windows, flared roofline, a centered wing, and of course, the hallmark of the Victorian age, a stout observation tower perched way up top.

Above: Only a few Second Empire carriage houses still exist throughout New Jersey, and this village contains three fine examples. Certainly referring to these structures as barns would have greatly offended their designers as they were completed to hold the finest carriages and wagons of the Victorian Age's fancy folk. They also make great playhouses, which the author can attest to having spent many fun afternoons in one in Keyport back in the '70s.

— Welcome to —

SANDY HOOK

est. 1764

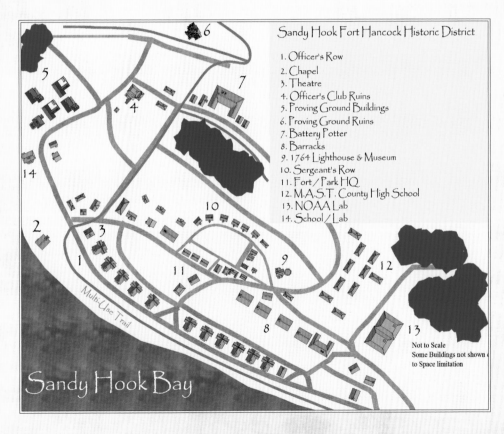

Sandy Hook Fort Hancock Historic District

1. Officer's Row
2. Chapel
3. Theatre
4. Officer's Club Ruins
5. Proving Ground Buildings
6. Proving Ground Ruins
7. Battery Potter
8. Barracks
9. 1764 Lighthouse & Museum
10. Sergeant's Row
11. Fort / Park HQ
12. M.A.S.T. County High School
13. NOAA Lab
14. School / Lab

Multi-Use Trail

Not to Scale
Some Buildings not shown
to Space limitation

Sandy Hook Bay

MIDDLETOWN, MONMOUTH COUNTY

The Leni Lenape had been using Sandy Hook as a hunting and gathering spot for centuries. The lands of the hook are plentiful in edible fruits, such as blueberry, huckleberry, beach plums, and the ever-abundant prickly pear cactus, which still grow along this seven-mile peninsula.

Native Americans also took great interest in the white-tailed deer, possums, muskrats, and skunks and spent much time fishing in the Horseshoe Cove area for fish, eels, turtles, and shellfish. Today, summer tourists spend most of their time hunting—not for game but for parking spaces in this popular National Recreation Area.

Here, among the sand and the cedars, the Hook was formed millions of years ago, first as a small island and later with northerly moving sands. It became the barrier peninsula that it is today, ever growing and changing with storms and ocean currents.

It was famed English explorer Henry Hudson who is credited with being the first white man to discover Sandy Hook on his third voyage. He anchored in the bay alongside a great sandy land while a massive forest fire was burning in the Navesink Highlands, no doubt the land that today encompasses Hartshorne Woods County Park. Hudson stayed in the bay for several days, and it is speculated that it was here that his party landed, consisting of three men and a crewman named John Colman. As they were exploring the area on foot, Colman was shot through the neck by an Indian's arrow and killed. Colman was buried by the crew of the half moon, below the sands and cedars in a place that was soon named Colman's Point, believed to be Sandy Hook, but debated to be Keansburg or even Staten Island.

It was to be almost a half century before any white man would again set foot on that land, which was now being referred to as Sandy Pointe by the Lenape. Part legend and part history, the story of Penelope Van Princes Stout is one of New Jersey's best. Her story is like many others in its beginning. While traveling to New Amsterdam in 1634, their ill-fated voyage is interrupted by a Nor'easter off the Jersey Coast. The ship, driven aground, breaks apart, and the survivors make it to the shore half-dead. Penelope and her husband, John Kent, survived as did the rest of the passengers. Kent had been sickened on the trip and was unable to leave with the rest of the passengers, who presumably had walked to Staten Island, promising to come back for the two left behind. Knowing that the Native Americans were not kind to the white man, Penelope and her husband were more or less left for dead by their shipmates.

Soon after they were abandoned, a group of Lenape came upon them and attacked, killing John with a hatchet, and upon turning on his wife partially scalped her and cut her open, exposing her entrails. The Lenape, believing she was dead, left, continuing on their way. Penelope did not die and was eventually found by another pair of Lenape, one of whom wanted to kill her; however, the elder Indian took her back to the camp near present-day Middletown Village and nursed her back to health. She lived with them for some time as a prisoner but was said to have been well cared for. Eventually, her shipmates had gotten word of a twenty-two-year-old white woman living among the Lenape, and they made the long trip to the village where they bartered her

The Half Moon. 1609.

It was on his ship, the *Half Moon,* that Hudson explored much of eastern coast of the United States in the summer of 1609. At that time, the only white settlement in the New World was that of Jamestown in Virginia. It was here at Sandy Poynte that legend tells us that while Hudson was anchored in the waters, his landing party was attacked, and John Colman was killed by the arrow from a Lenape Warrior protecting his prized hunting grounds. (The National Archives)

release. Penelope later married Richard Stout, returned to the future site of Middletown and helped found the town. Penelope lived until 1732 and was buried in a long-lost grave somewhere in the vicinity of Middletown and Holmdel. Sadly, the home that she spent the last years of her life, at 73 Everett Road in Holmdel, was demolished in 2003; the house was one of the best examples of a frame Dutch style house in New Jersey. Stout lived for 110 years and is the descendant to thousands of Stouts in America today.

In 1764, construction was completed on the Sandy Hook lighthouse and adjacent keeper's quarters. Built to protect ships from the dangerous shoals and false hook sandbar leading into New York harbor, the lighthouse was the scene of a two-hour battle in May of 1776 after the lighthouse had fallen into British hands.

British Troops took possession of Sandy Hook in 1776 and continued to occupy it until the end of the war. Patriots attempted

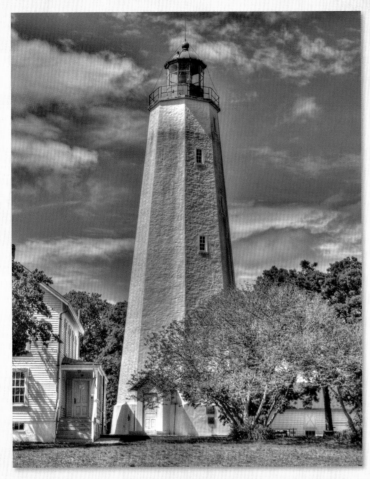

Designed by architect Isaac Conroe, the Sandy Hook Lighthouse was completed and lit for the first time in 1764. America's inspiraton of independence still stands today as an active navigational beacon , powered by a ten-inch 1,000 watt light bulb. It has guided the way for countless ships since being lit and was restored in 2000 by the National Park Service.

Hook to obtain fresh water. They did not return and were presumed to have deserted, which occurred often, apparently.

The Captain of the HMS *Assistance* ordered 1st Lieutenant Hamilton Douglas Halyburton to take some men on a search party and round up the deserters. Halyburton and his men were soon caught in a terrible snowstorm and were found three days later, frozen to death; the fate of the deserters was never known. Halyburton and his men were buried in a common grave near Horseshoe Cove.

Later, his mother, Katherine, the Countess Dowager of Morton, erected a large marble monument in memoriam of her son and his men. In 1808, a group of French Sailors landed on Sandy Hook and destroyed the monument; the story disappeared from memory and did not reappear until a century later. While the Army was engaged in widening the roadway the skeletal remains of the crew were once again located. They were reinterred in Cypress Hills Cemetery in Queens, New York. It would not be until 1937 that a permanent monument would be erected to their memory.

By the first decade of the nineteenth century, Sandy Hook was a major point of fortification for the supposed impending British Invasion. It was in 1807 that a large fort was first erected overlooking the bay. Today, no trace remains of this fortification, known as Fort Gates; it is believed that it was removed sometime between 1850 and 1890. Archaeological work in the 1980s found many military items dating from the war of 1812 at the former site of the fort, placed somewhere behind Officer Row house 21 in the parade ground.

Sandy Hook would experience much growth through the nineteenth century: In 1857, construction started on a massive granite Fort, sometimes known as Fort Hudson or Fort Lincoln. Under construction for nearly twelve years, the fort was never completed after millions of dollars were expended on its construction. Today, most of the northeast wall exists along the ocean, and one large corner caisson exists as the base for the water tower. Several arches with iron shutters, once built to conceal large Rodman guns, stand frozen in time and hidden away in the briars, brush, and poison ivy of the Hook's back roads.

As time went on, Sandy Hook became the birthplace of the United States Lifesaving Service in 1848. The first USLS station was built in Spermaceti Cove at that time and was moved in the 1950s to Twin Lights

to blow the lighthouse up at least once, but it would not budge, and they soon retreated. The war had ended on September 3, 1783, but it took some time for the defeated British fleet anchored in Sandy Hook Bay to pick up anchor and sail back to England. On December 30 and 31, 1783, a total of eleven British soldiers had rowed to Sandy

State Park. By 1874, the place was transformed into the US Army proving ground and, in 1895, was joined by Fort Hancock, two major military bases that operated side by side, albeit independently, for many years.

Sandy Hook and the Horseshoe Cove area became a major railroad and steamboat hub to New York City beginning in the mid 1860s. The Central Railroad of New Jersey constructed a huge wharf, enclosed passenger waiting sheds, warehouses, railroad bunkhouses, and even a turntable to spin the trains around and send them back south. Later, the site was forced to close by the US Army, who felt that it was too dangerous to the passengers since it was located downrange from the proving grounds' giant guns. The railroad moved the entire operation to Atlantic Highlands in 1892.

Today, only a few pilings and bricks from the roundhouse survive along the bayside beach to tell the forgotten story of the Steamboat Wharf. By the 1940s Fort Hancock, the US Coast Guard, National Weather Service, and a host of other federal operations existed on the peninsula. In 1962, the southern portion of the property was transferred to the state and Sandy Hook State Park was created.

Fort Hancock, once home to thousands of soldiers, their families, and civilian workers, was deactivated in 1972 after three centuries of army occupation. It was transferred to the National Park Service. Although early legislation had created Sandy Hook National Seashore, it was absorbed into the larger Gateway National Recreation Area project, which began in 1974. Fort Hancock received designation as a National Historic District in 1981. Sandy Hook is undoubtedly one of the most historic spots in the nation, and it is hoped that someday it will be recognized for its worthy contribution to our independence, becoming a designated National Historical Park.

Visitor Information

Visiting Sandy Hook is beautiful all year long. During summer months plan to wait in long lines and pass through the National Park Service Fee station; however, if you are strictly visiting Fort Hancock, the fee is waived. The lighthouse is open daily for tours throughout the summer months and on weekends throughout the year. As of this publication, the Visitor Center at Spermaceti Cove is still closed from damages from Hurricane Sandy in 2012. The Visitor Center (732-872-5970) is now located in the Lighthouse Keepers Quarters at Mercer and Hudson Roads. Plan to spend several hours, or several years, exploring all of the history of the place, and watch out for poison ivy—it is waiting for you everywhere.

For a quick side trip, be sure to visit the former Highlands Army Defense Sites (HAADS), located on Portland Road in Monmouth County's Hartshorne Woods Park. The MCPS recently obtained, restored, and remounted one sixteen-inch gun that provided coastal defenses throughout World War II. The gun barrel was originally mounted on the USS *New Jersey* during WWII and was donated by the US Navy to the Park System. Here this massive concrete bunker, known as Battery Lewis, mirrors two other near-identical ones at Sandy Hook, Batteries Kingman and Mills. www.nps.gov/gate/planyourvisit/sandy-hook-hours.htm

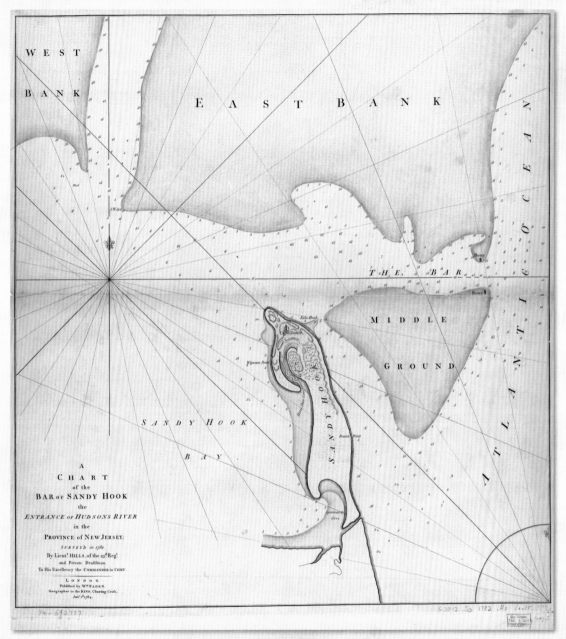

A
CHART
of the
BAR of SANDY HOOK
the
ENTRANCE of HUDSONS RIVER
in the
PROVINCE of NEW JERSEY;
SURVEYD in 1781.
By Lieut! HILLS, of the 23? Reg!
and Private Draftsman
To His Excellency the COMMANDER in CHIEF.

LONDON.
Published by W.™ FADEN,
Geographer to the KING, Charing-Cross,
Jan.™ 1.™ 1784.

In 1782, this British military map was completed for Her Majesty's Navy who continually occupied New York Harbor. The location of the lighthouse is clearly shown along with both Horseshoe and Spermaceti Coves. Two other locations shown, Wigwam Point and Brant's Point, have been lost to obscurity. At this time the ocean had cut into the Shrewsbury River allowing the hook to become an island; this inlet had closed up by 1830.

Not much is known of Fort Gates as it had vanished before photography began. A rudimentary plan of the place resides in the National Archives, which shows a five-pointed fort of this design already in place. The fort, constructed before the War of 1812, was at the ready to protect the entrance to New York harbor from another naval invasion.

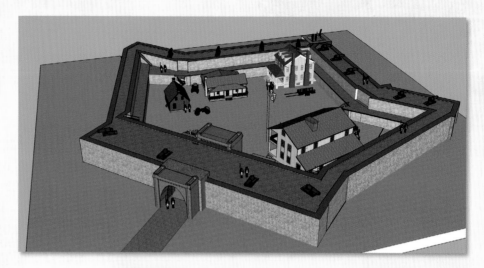

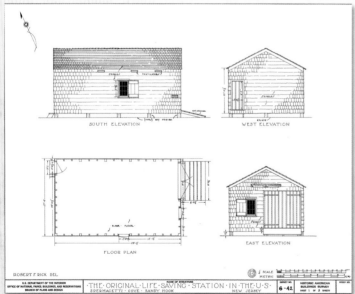

Once upon a time, before there was a US Coast Guard, there was a US Lifesaving Service. Comprised of local men who staffed the stations along the coast at various intervals, they were instrumental in saving thousands of lives from a watery grave. Begun at Sandy Hook in 1848, the Spermaceti Cove Station was the first of a network that circled the entire nation's coastal waters. It was relocated to Twin Lights State Park far above its original home in the 1950s. (The Library of Congress)

Costing several million dollars, the massive granite star Fort Lincoln was begun in 1857, with work ending in 1869 before it was ever completed. Most of the Fort still remains encased in concrete from the building of the Nine Gun battery in 1899–1901. Many parts of the grand Civil War are totally unknown to historians and visitors alike; arches, staircases, and walls still remain hidden in the poison ivy and dune grass.

The ruins at Sandy Hook are extensive and, unfortunately, the result of a lack of funds and forty years of deferred maintenance. This complex of brick warehouses was constructed after a devastating fire reduced the original ones to ashes. One way to differentiate buildings from the Sandy Hook Proving Grounds from those at Fort Hancock are the colors of brick: red is Proving Ground, yellow is Fort Hancock.

Some may guess this fire hydrant was dumped into the ocean; however, it is a part of the last remains of the US Army's secret communications area that once covered this locale. The buildings and lands have long eroded by Atlantic storms over the last fifty years.

One of the best examples of Second Empire architecture in the area is the nearly collapsed Officer's Club. Built as the office and residence of the Commander of the Proving Ground in 1877–1878, it became the O-Club before World War II. Rock legend Bruce Springsteen, a familiar visitor to the Hook, filmed the video for "Brilliant Disguise" there in 1987. Today it is in imminent collapse.

The impressive fortification known as Battery Pottery was constructed of concrete in 1893, along the east side of Fort Hancock. The giant casement houses two steam-powered disappearing cannons that would rise up, fire, and then retract into the casement to be reloaded. Although powerful, it was deemed unsuccessful and removed in 1906. Though crumbling, it stands today open for tours. (The Library of Congress)

All of Fort Hancock's buff-colored brick Officers' Quarters were constructed in 1898–1899 and face Sandy Hook bay. Built of a typical Army design, the eighteen nearly identical quarters were spared no expense when built, each containing double front parlors, large pantries, and three floors of living space. Three of them have been rehabilitated with the remainder to be rebuilt when funding allows.

Since the earliest of times, visitors have been drawn to the ruins of their forefathers. The crumbling pieces of our past are both intriguing and disheartening at the same time. The often photographed 1907 Proving Grounds buildings are slowly being reclaimed by nature.

A paid fire department has existed within the confines of Sandy Hook since 1874. The first steam fire engine in Monmouth County was placed in service here in 1876. Firehouse No. 2 was built in 1910 and used until 1952. It was used for a variety of activities over the next sixty years. In 2012, after Firehouse No. 1 was destroyed in Hurricane Sandy, this building was reactivated for seven months as an active firehouse and was staffed twenty-four hours a day.

Just as all of the residents and our families were evacuating Sandy Hook, we stopped to capture the 1893 Lifesaving Station just twenty hours before Hurricane Sandy made landfall. Forty-eight hours later, we reentered the park to find it virtually destroyed by a massive tidal surge; what wasn't washed away was badly damaged. The Lifesaving Station survived; though gutted, it has been closed pending repairs. The building had served as Parks Visitor Center for nearly forty years.

— Welcome to —

ALLAIRE AND PHALANX

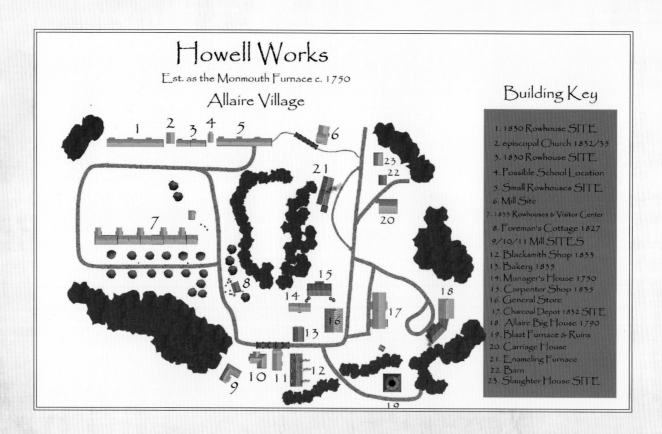

Howell Works

Est. as the Monmouth Furnace c. 1750

Allaire Village

Building Key

1. 1830 Rowhouse SITE
2. Episcopal Church 1832/35
3. 1830 Rowhouse SITE
4. Possible School Location
5. Small Rowhouses SITE
6. Mill Site
7. 1833 Rowhouses & Visitor Center
8. Foreman's Cottage 1827
9/10/11 Mill SITES
12. Blacksmith Shop 1833
13. Bakery 1835
14. Manager's House 1750
15. Carpenter Shop 1835
16. General Store
17. Charcoal Depot 1832 SITE
18. Allaire Big House 1790
19. Blast Furnace & Ruins
20. Carriage House
21. Enameling Furnace
22. Barn
23. Slaughter House SITE

HOWELL WORKS AT ALLAIRE VILLAGE
est. 1750
WALL TOWNSHIP, MONMOUTH COUNTY

Likely built by Isaac Palmer, this four-bedroom frame dwelling is the oldest existing building in Allaire. Completed about 1750, during the time Palmer opened his sawmill along the nearby banks of the Manasquan River, it was used as the manager's house for both the Monmouth Furnace and the Howell Works.

In 1889, author Gustave Kobbe said of Allaire, "The most extensive and picturesque ruins of this kind are at Allaire, where only the stack still standing among the pines may be seen, a pathetic reminder of the spirit of enterprise which created the place . . ." As early as 1750, the area of Southern Shrewsbury Township (later Howell, now Wall) was the site of a sawmill that had been built by Isaac Palmer and Samuel Swain along the head of the Manasquan River. The site flourished and within a few years two bog iron operations were begun in the area; the Williamsburg Forge appeared around 1803, while Monmouth Furnace was begun in 1812–1813. The area with its low-lying accessible streams were perfect for harvesting bog iron just like its counterparts Martha Furnace, Etna Furnace, and the dozens of others that dotted the landscape in the Pines. For an in-depth look at these industries, Arthur Pierce's 1957 work, *Iron in the Pines* is highly recommended.

By 1821, Monmouth Furnace consisted of fifteen houses, the manager's house, furnace, sawmill, and other village buildings. The property at this time was leased to Benjamin Howell of Philadelphia who was a business partner of James P. Allaire, a successful New York City foundry owner. Allaire decided to purchase the furnace site in 1822 for $19,000; this purchase included all structures, the furnace, and 5,000 acres of pines and mixed hardwood forest. Allaire quickly went about developing a plan to enlarge the village and modernize productivity over the next two decades. Allaire's reputation as a perfectionist as a businessman and a benefactor to his workers was to be carried over from his Manhattan offices to the forests of Monmouth County in just a few short years.

The bog iron industry was a labor intensive operation. Ore raisers were the men who went into the streams and wetlands digging the clumped iron masses and loading them into shallow draft boats to

be towed back as near as possible to the furnace. Colliers worked day and night to burn the wood down to hard charcoal to be used in the smelting process; some other vanished worker titles in 1824 included ore-carters, woodsetters, coal drawers, and wood-wheelers. In all, over forty-one titles and 200 workers made the village work.

The furnace itself used a large chimney (or a stack, as it was called in this profession) to heat up and liquefy the iron, removing it from the other organic matter that it clung to. After the iron was heated, it would drain into cut-out areas of the furnace house, shaped like a pig and its sucklings, hence the term pig iron. The pig iron would be cooled and later taken through a series of processes before it would be heated again and put into casts and molds for implements. The 1824 list of Allaire patterns included kettles, pots, pans, spiders, flasks, tea kettles, and Franklin stoves. For his village work, Allaire went about building an almost entirely new town on the site of Monmouth Furnace; when completed, it housed over 300 workers and their families. The village became one of the largest industrial company towns in New Jersey by 1831, when the Howell Works US post office began accepting customers. Four stories of goods and merchandise were carried in the brick General Store, which was said to have been the largest of its type when completed in 1835; the store was not only utilized by the Howell Works employees but the farmers from Howell Township and other areas.

The Howell Works furnace stayed in continued operation (blast) until 1837 and then sporadically after that until 1845. New technologies in iron ore moved away from the bog iron method, preferring to utilize new iron deposits in Pennsylvania and the western frontier. The Furnace fires were extinguished for the last time in '45 and the village slowed down a bit after that. About half the population moved on to other places, and while some stayed to farm or work outside the village limit, the heyday of the Howell Works had slipped into the past. The entire property was surveyed and advertised for sale in 1855; when no buyer came forward, James Allaire retained ownership of the place until his death in 1858. From this time on,

Allaire's son, Hal, became the owner and caretaker of the place. Hal was born in the village in 1847 and was just eleven when his father died. He was an accomplished architect, painter, and surveyor, and graduated from Columbia University in 1869, soon returning to live with his mother in the Big House.

After his mother died in 1879, Hal continued to live in the Big House while the rest of the village slowly crumbled, brick by brick, building by building. Hal slipped away in 1901, in the same home he was born in.

In 1890, the former Carpenter Shop was remodeled by William Delisle into the Allaire Inn, a once-famous Jersey Shore restaurant and inn that operated from 1890 to 1915. It was one of the few buildings that Hal allowed to be renovated.

It was during the time of the Allaire Inn that property first was called the Deserted Village of (at) Allaire. Travelers arriving by car or by train strolled the grounds to see the once-bustling village empty and overgrown, streets clogged with vines and underbrush, and the Christ Church windowless and forgotten. Word spread of the Deserted Village and it soon occupied a place on state road maps and guidebooks.

The property passed into the hands of famed New York City journalist Arthur Brisbane in 1907; Brisbane allowed the continued operation of the Allaire Inn and, in 1929, allowed the Monmouth Council of Boy Scouts to utilize the village as Camp Burton. Over the next decade, thousands of New Jersey Scouts spent summers and winters at the camp learning survival skills, becoming good scouts and worshipping in the Christ Church, which they restored in 1930, slowly bringing life back to the old village. Millionaire Brisbane charged the scouts only $1 annually to lease the property. Buildings were repaired and whitewashed, roads were cleared and graded, and the millpond was repaired and flooded for the camp swimming hole.

Brisbane, inspired by the success of the camp and realizing the historical significance of the place, had decided to deed the property to the Department of Conservation and Development in the early 1930s as the state's first historic park. Brisbane died in 1936 before this could be completed, and camp Burton closed in 1940 at the onset of World War II.

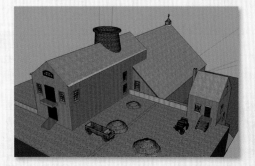

The massive four-story blasting furnace house and casting shed was put into operation about 1830. It was the largest and most important structure in the village, where the bog iron was taken to be smelted, refined, cast, and cured. At its height, dozens of men worked in the hot, smoky building, which was layered with floors of windows for natural lighting during those long winter days. The building had completely collapsed by 1890 and most likely suffered a fire at some point, which hastened its demise.

By 1940, the first 1,200 acres became state property and, while severely delayed by both World War II and the Korean War, Allaire State Park finally welcomed its first visitors through the tollbooth in 1957.

James Allaire would be proud of the park and historic village that reflected on his life's work over the past half-century. Beginning in the 1960s, keen interest in our cultural heritage was amplified with the impending nations bicentennial in 1976. Allaire Village began to receive funds to stabilize and restore many of the buildings, including the Blacksmith Shop, which had been reduced to a windowless shell. It was meticulously restored in 1961, and today few can tell that it is a restoration. A visit to Allaire, for many, is an annual pilgrimage: Visits to the General Store for stick candy, cookies at the bakery, and the smell and sounds of the Blacksmith Shop truly are an iconic New Jersey day trip. An important part of the park is the Pine Creek Railroad, located just outside the village limits. The narrow gauge railroad was constructed here in 1959–1965 to allow a complete steam-powered train excursion to operate in conjunction with the park. Today, the New Jersey Transportation Museum operates both steam and diesel powered equipment throughout most of the year to the delight of rail fans and five-year-olds alike!

Many buildings at Allaire were planned to be reconstructed in the park's master plan created in the 1960s; to date only two have been rebuilt. The Blacksmith Shop (as noted) and the front row houses (all but two, which had collapsed by 1900) were rebuilt to original plans in 1985. Today, they house the visitor center and expansive Howell Work's museum and research library.

Allaire's Church is quite unique in that the bell and clock tower are located on the pulpit end of the building. This was required after the 1836 addition, which doubled the building's size, and during its renovation it was discovered that the older section could not bear the weight of the new tower. So the backward church at Allaire was finished, leading many to wonder if the back was the front once! Today, the Christ Church is often the scene of spring and fall wedding and memorial services.

The Deserted Village of Allaire has lived an ever changing life, first as an early sawmill site, then a company town, popular Boy Scout Camp, World War I army training ground, and finally a State Park. In the entire life of the village it was only truly deserted from 1940 until 1957 while funds were being set aside to restore the park.

Allaire State Park today consists of more than 5,000 acres of forest, campgrounds, hiking trails, and of course, the village itself, managed by the non-profit Historic Village at Allaire Association, who works to ensure that it continues to be one of the best living history sites in the nation.

Visitor Information

Allaire State Park and its village are located on 4265 Atlantic Avenue (NJ County Road 524), just off Interstate 195 in Wall Townships. The park has no permanent food facilities; however, ice cream, hot dog, and other vendors can be found in the parking lot seasonally. The park office can be reached at 732-938-2371 or by visiting, https://allairevillage.org/. The Village has special events all year long, so check the calendar before visiting. The Allenwood General Store, located just east of the park entrance, is a longtime favorite to get drinks and lunch (and of course the best Pork Roll around). The Pine Creek Railroad is open daily in the summer months and on weekends and during special events throughout the year. They can be reached by visiting www.njmt.org/ or by calling (732) 938-5524. The park also has a campground with trailer sites, yurts, and cabins that fill up quickly. Allaire is additionally a starting point for traveling, hiking, or biking on the Edgar Felix Trail, which runs five-plus miles from the park into the Borough of Manasquan.

The foreman for the Howell Works lived in this tidy brick dwelling along the Main Village Road beginning in 1829. It consists of one room on the first floor and one on the second with a large cooking and heating fireplace along the north wall. During the era of the Boy Scouts, it was occupied as their first aid station.

Today, the main village passes by the Foreman's Cottage; however, the original road passes by the rear and accounts for the more front-door symmetrical appearance on the east side of the dwelling. The traces of the original road are still clearly visible.

This photographic reconstruction highlights just how little the Village Store has changed since being built c. 1835. The store served as the mercantile center of both Wall and Howell Townships during its heyday. It closed in 1846 and was used as a small factory for different concerns for decades. Famous for its hard stick flavored candy, harmonicas, and train whistles, it is doubtful any parent has ever made it out of the store empty handed.

This view of the village looking west, shows from left to right: the 1835 blacksmith shop, the general store, the manager's house, and the carpenter shop. With the exception of the manager's house, these three buildings were among the first to be restored.

By the time this postcard was made in 1915, all but two of the 1829 rowhouses had completely collapsed. The two remaining rowhouses had been occupied by tenants since the village closed and was taken over by the Boy Scouts as the camp headquarters in 1929. In 1985, the State of New Jersey rebuilt the missing nine rowhouses, turning this into the visitor center and park museum.

One of the best parts of this Jersey ghost town is the chance to stop by the bakery. True to its original purpose, the bakery, built in 1835, still sells a fantastic assortment of sweets and breads. Although they are no longer prepared in the rear beehive oven, it would not be uncommon for people to travel far distances in the fog and rain to just catch the aroma of this place.

An integral part of any village during the nineteenth century was the blacksmith shop and foundry. James Allaire built this place of business in 1835 near the gristmill. When the State took over the property, the blacksmith shop had been converted into a large storage building, as most of its original walls had long since collapsed. Restored in 1961, it has been continually used by blacksmiths to demonstrate the trade.

Allaire's All Saints Episcopal Church was built in two sections: the first in 1832 and the front part in 1835. Unlike Feltville, Allaire did not require worship of his employees; however, attendance at Sunday services was expected. It has been restored several times over the centuries and is still actively used for ceremonies throughout the year. Note the original clock, which continues to keep accurate time.

The park held a large assortment of period carriages and wagons, which were stored in various buildings. This four-wheeled Surrey was popular for a good part of the nineteenth and twentieth century and was the equivalent of today's minivan. Seating for six and a cargo area in the back made this wagon a rural necessity. Allaire's Surrey has been stripped of its interior.

The carpenter shop and enameling furnace are the last two buildings that proudly wear their white-washed coats of paint as they did in 1840. The carpenter shop was transformed into the Allaire Inn in 1890 and continued as a popular restaurant for nearly forty years.

All of the seasons at the village are special; however, it seems to really come alive in the fall. As the humid airs of summer blow away, pumpkins and Halloween festivities take its place. The nearby narrow gauge Pine Creek Railroad steam engine's smoke fills the air and makes for a most excellent adventure on a brisk Saturday.

I doubt that the state rangers would have approved of these youths scaling the walls of the old furnace stack. Yet to be restored in this late 1950s postcard, the furnace would soon be repaired, missing bricks replaced, and have a large roof placed over it.

Welcome to

PHALANX

est. 1845

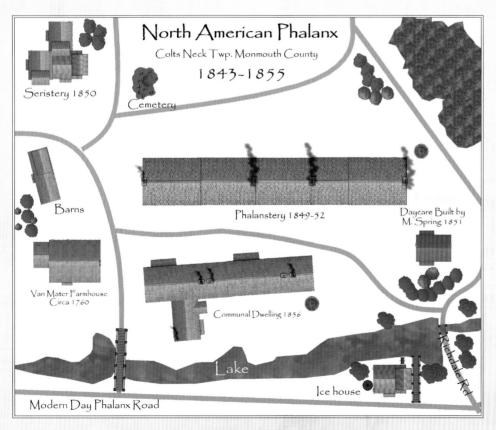

North American Phalanx
Colts Neck Twp. Monmouth County
1843–1855

Seristery 1850

Cemetery

Barns

Van Mater Farmhouse
Circa 1760

Phalanstery 1849–52

Daycare Built by
M. Spring 1851

Communal Dwelling 1856

Lake

Richdale Rd

Ice house

Modern Day Phalanx Road

COLTS NECK TOWNSHIP, MONMOUTH COUNTY

It was during the early 1840s that a new idea was found to be spreading across the country: the idea of self-contained utopian communities. The ideals of this movement were focused on the beliefs of Frenchman Charles Fourier, a wealthy aristocrat born in 1772. Fourier had developed a self-proclaimed utopian society free of the civilized world, where all persons would receive pay based upon skill, whether male or female. He proclaimed these odd little places should be called Phalanxes, where the residents would live in specific four-story phalanstères, with the wealthiest living on the top floors and the common people on the street level. The term "Phalanx" was derived from the Greek language and means firmness of union. Though Fourier had already died by the time this idea was embraced in our nation, it had been resurrected by leading New York City socialites. Albert Brisbane and newspaper publisher Horace Greeley led the so-called Fourierist Movement at the time and soon found a group of people who were willing to pledge membership to this new agricultural commune. This group was led by Charles Sears and Nathan Starks, two of the followers of the movement, and they began organizing the new North American Phalanx.

Investors were located, and by 1843, 643 acres, known as the Van Mater Farm, were purchased in Atlantic Township, New Jersey (today's Colts Neck) for $14,000. By September of that year, the first twelve families moved into the Phalanx and began occupying two existing houses, one of which was the Daniel Polhemus house built around 1730, according the Historic America Building Survey completed in 1941. By 1847, the main phalanstères was completed along with a sawmill, blacksmith shop, and a steam-powered machine shop, grist mill, and other buildings. As with any rural community, horse stables, corn cribs, and ice houses, as well as other outbuildings, were built and ready for use as early as 1845. In keeping with Fourier's plan, the new village contained a school and what may have been the state's first dedicated children's day care. The day care was an important part of the Phalanx operation as women were dutifully engaged in village life, whether working in agriculture or with domestic duties, a mother's full attention was to be paid at the task at hand and not watching over those little ones! It has been said that the Phalanx was a century ahead of the rest of the world; the group established profit-sharing, the thirty-hour work week, equal pay for both women and men, planned recreation, and a healthy economy without currency—all of which existed through cooperation and religious tolerance.

The Phalanx continued to grow and at its peak, between 1847 and 1854, was home to over 150 persons all living and working in one huge dormitory. The hallmark of the Phalanx was the massive phalanstère where nearly everyone lived, relaxed in parlors or dayrooms, and ate harmoniously in a seventy-foot-long dining hall. It is important to note that the Phalanx was a non-religious, non-denominational commune, and it is said that the Quakers, Baptists, Christians, Jews, and even Atheists worked side by side to help the

THE NORTH AMERICAN PHALANSTERY.

This c. 1850 view of the village appeared in a lithograph as a circulated advertisement. In it we can still clearly see the Van Mater home; next is the Phalanstery, along with the attached boarding house completed in 1849. Also the Carpenter Gothic Childcare Center sits to the right of the main building. (The Library of Congress)

community grow and prosper. Through its rich soil and experimental agricultural methods the village did just that and turned a profit annually from 1843 to 1850. Most of the fruits and vegetables from the village were taken by wagon to the wharves in Red Bank and Keyport, loaded on to steamers, such as the *Holmdel* and the *Magenta,* later being off-loaded to the New York City Markets after the trip across the Raritan Bay. One of the industries here was the manufacturer of black silk stockings, which wound up being worn all over the world!

Governance of the Phalanx was by a unique and complex system that was far advanced for its day. All trades would be split into "series," which were then subdivided again by groups. All trades elected a chief, who was responsible for recording performance of those assigned to him, deciding on pay for performance and reporting back to the council. Unique to the village at the time, the toughest jobs received the best pay while easy work was compensated the least!

Peace and tranquility were not long enjoyed at the Phalanx. In 1854, a new Fourier Society was being organized in Perth Amboy known as the Raritan Bay Union. It soon attracted some of the leading tradesmen of the Phalanx, including the master carpenter. Suspiciously, the sawmill burned to the ground on September 10, 1854, and with no insurance on the mill, the village plummeted even further into debt.

Within a year the Phalanx had voted to disband, and the property was sold off lot by lot, and the commune members moved on by the close of 1856.

Over the next century, many of the structures of the Phalanx were moved or torn down for lumber and rebuilt elsewhere. Somehow the main phalanstère built in 1855 survived for many years as a busy hotel between Red Bank and Freehold. For nearly a century the former village property was owned by the Bucklin family who retained ownership through 1944. Eventually abandoned, it became a hangout for local teens as a party site. In 1970, the building was donated to the Monmouth Museum; however, nothing was done with the property and in 1972, after a last minute attempt by the Colts Neck Historical Society to purchase it, it was sadly destroyed in a spectacular fire.

About one month after the fire, a letter came from Washington, DC, announcing that the building had been approved to be listed on the National Register of Historic Places. Never rebuilt, the memory of Phalanx exists today in a few converted homes, namely the Gothic style day care, the post office, and two township thoroughfares—Bucklin Road and Phalanx Road. Nearby, overlooking the Swimming River Reservoir is the grave of the community's treasurer, John B. Angell, who, in 1855, purchased one of the village lots when it was subdivided. Mr. Angell, remained living there until his death and chose to be buried there where he keeps an eternal eye over the old village from this knoll.

Visitor Information

Phalanx isn't a park or a village or much of anything today; however, you can find one Commemorative sign along Phalanx Road near its intersection with Richdale Road. A few original structures remain along Phalanx Road, including the Post Office. Turning on to Richdale and then onto Bucklin Road, you view the Child Day Center, which is the well-preserved Stick Style house set far back from the road. The grave of John Angell can be reached by a trail that runs off a small pull-off on Bucklin Road, often inhabited by Fisherman looking for a catch from the Swimming River Reservoir.

The childcare center of Phalanx was completed in 1850 in the Carpenter Gothic style which had reached its pinnacle. The building is the only structure remaining of the original village complex on its original foundation. It is today a private home and in remarkable condition.

John Angell, arrived in the fledgling commune of Phalanx in 1855. As the community's treasurer, Angell was devoted to the place and remained a resident long after the Phalanx had faded. He died in July of 1895 and was buried in the family spot, which today stands on a bluff overlooking the Swimming River Reservoir.

By 1965, the Phalanstery had been vacant for some time. It had yet to be vandalized and was living on borrowed time. Within a few short years, relic hunters had stripped every window and nearly every door from the building. Just as it was finally about to be saved, a suspicious fire leveled the place in 1972. (The Library of Congress)

Welcome to
GREENWICH LANDING
Settled 1684

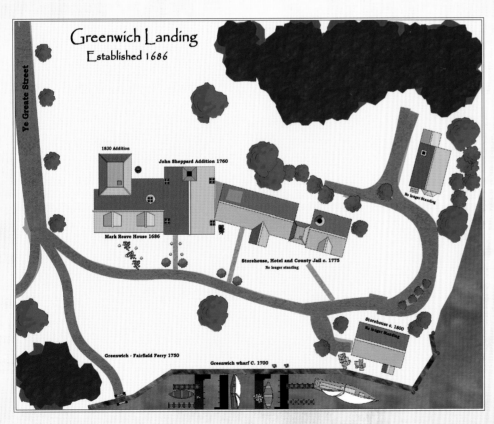

Greenwich Landing
Established 1686

Ye Greate Street

1830 Addition

John Sheppard Addition 1760

Mark Reave House 1686

No longer Standing

Storehouse, Hotel and County Jail c. 1775
No longer standing

Storehouse c. 1800
No longer Standing

Greenwich - Fairfield Ferry 1750

Greenwich wharf C. 1700

GREENWICH TOWNSHIP, CUMBERLAND COUNTY

First settled in 1686, the Cumberland County Village of Greenwich is home to about 400 people all living on just a few shaded streets along the banks of the Cohansey River. Walking the streets of Greenwich is akin to feeling as if you have been transported back in time to a Charles Dickens novel—and unlike anything else in New Jersey. When down this way, make sure you pronounce it "Green-Witch," for no one in this vicinity wants it confused with its namesake in England! Greenwich appears in this book because of its major importance in our state's history, and though not a true ghost town in its own right, the most historic spot in the town is the old landing area at the very end of Ye Greate Street. It is here, at the end of this very ancient road, that you come to a large brick structure, noticeably vacant for decades, but with some restoration work occurring at times. You won't find the place in any National Park Service guides, and it isn't even maintained by the state, even though the history and folklore of the location is the fabric from which our country's independence was woven.

Originally, the property was purchased by English Quaker Mark Reeve, who had recently arrived from England to escape religious persecution. In 1675, Reeve traveled to the New World aboard the brig, the *Griffin,* along with John Fenwick, the founder of Salem, and William Penn, whose connection with our nation's history needs no introduction.

They arrived in early summer of 1675 and went about laying out a new town along the Cohansey River, near the Delaware Bay. By 1684, Reeve purchased the first plot of land in the new tract and began erecting a two-story brick dwelling (McMahon 1964). During this time, Greenwich was part of Salem County and would remain so until Cumberland was created in January of 1748, at which time Greenwich became the county seat. This title was short lived; by the end of the year Bridgeton became the new home for county government.

The old landing was the site of a brief skirmish in 1748, when the French and Spanish privateers captured several British ships, entered Delaware Bay, and took twenty-seven prisoners in a boat, and then docked at Greenwich. What became of the prisoners has been lost over the years. This, though, would not be the last event at the old Greenwich wharf to be recorded.

One of the most brazen stories in the pages of Revolutionary New Jersey history occurred just before Christmas 1774. As the icy winds blew off the Cohansey River one December evening, a large brig under British flag docked at the wharf to resupply before heading to her destination in Philadelphia.

Captain Allen, who was commanding the *Greyhound* with a cargo of precious East India tea, took anchor alongside the small sloops at the ferry landing. Captain Allen knew of the hostilities toward England and her taxation policies of goods, especially tea, so he made arrangements to off-load the precious bales of tea to a secret location far away from those with patriotic ideas. Allen had knowledge that another brig with a cargo of tea had been harassed at Philadelphia and not allowed to dock a few weeks earlier. Ole'

The oldest section of the Reeve-Sheppard house dates to c. 1684 and was constructed in the popular Georgian Style. John Sheppard purchased the place from Quaker Minister Thomas Chalkey in 1760. Sheppard then went about building an entirely new house onto the original in the Adam style which doubled the size of the place. It has remained virtually unchanged since.

The Reeve – Sheppard House has been quietly watching the Cohansey and its tides since it was completed in 1684. The early architecture of this house could be described as an interesting marriage of Georgian and Dutch with touch of federal influence on the new addition. The structure today is in a state of neglect and it is hoped that preservation funds can be found to save, what is certainly, one of the oldest private homes in our nation.

This first storehouse was in use long before America had gained her independence. Adjacent to the storehouse (obscured by the tree) is the small stone gaol, as it was known in the early days of Greenwich. The storehouse and jail were photographed just in time for the HABS in 1933, as they soon vanished; no trace remains of them today. (The Library of Congress)

This c. 1955 postcard shows the house in finer days, freshly painted in a coat of bright white. The back of the card reads "This was the first house built by a Quaker settler. Adjacent to the Cohansey, it personifies the fact that our long forgotten rivers were once important transportation arteries. Our sleepy Cohansey River was once an important lifeline with not only England, but the orient as well."

Captain Allen had gotten word that a trusted loyalist, Daniel Bowen, lived in Greenwich, and he was contacted to hide the tea in his cellar.

The good folks of Cumberland County selected thirty-five Cumberland loyalists to assist in moving and storing the tea to Bowen's Cellar at the house on Roadstown-Greenwich Road, a little more than three miles from the landing. With the tea safely stored, the loyalists returned home to their warm keeping rooms. Of course, not every resident was a loyalist; in fact, so many patriots were in the area that it didn't take long for a plan to form, fueled by the Boston incident just a year before. As the sun set on Thursday, December 22, 1774, a large group of youths dressed as Indians raided Bowen's Cellar and carted the entire cargo to the market Square. Here the tea provided the kindling to a history-making bonfire that infuriated the loyalists.

A trial was held by handpicked jurors who returned a no cause for action for the thirty-five "Indians," one of whom, Richard Howell, became the third governor of the state just twenty years later!

It is recorded that in the warm spring of 1778 what is known as The Greenwich Horror occurred. It appears that Captain Dan Bowen, the same from the tea incident, told that while a group of British troops were encamped at the landing, a huge, hairy beast emerged from the Cohansey and devoured Privates Jason White and George Chandler. (Taniguchi/*South Jersey Times,* October 16, 2012.)

Visitor Information

When you finally arrive in Greenwich, you will feel miles away from the rest of New Jersey and the twenty-first century. There isn't much traffic along the few streets in town: folks coming and going to the post office or eating at the town's only restaurant on Ye Greate Street; two Quaker meeting houses, one for summer, one for winter; a Methodist and a Baptist church; and the village firehouse make up much of the downtown—which is pretty much the entire town. Passing the businesses and heading east along Ye Greate Street you will arrive at the landing area. To your right will be the ancient Mark Reeve house, standing for four centuries along the muddy banks of the peacefully silent Cohansey River to explore its history is a journey back in time.

Not much remains of the once-busy Port of Greenwich today: the docks, storehouses, and ferry have long been swallowed by the waves; however, the home stands solid. It should be noted that the property is private and abuts other private homes, so make arrangements or stop by the neighbors to say hello when visiting. Missing from the property is the stone storehouse and first Cumberland County Jail, which was erected here in c. 1660. The building was photographed and measured during the Historic American Building Survey in 1933 and was in derelict condition even then. It stood just to the north of the main house facing the river and had vanished by the 1940s.

In 1908, the Cumberland County Historical Society erected this monument to commemorate the infamous Greenwich Tea Party. It was erected in the village market square on the very spot that the rebellion burned that precious cargo on the evening of December 22, 1774. On it are the names of the known participants, including future New Jersey Governor Richard Howell.

Near this very spot, the *Greyhound* docked in 1774 with her cargo of teas that were most likely bound for Philadelphia. The old wharf has mostly disappeared except for a few ancient pilings and some ancient barns that still stand. From here the small dinghy's shone their blue and yellow signal lamps to assist escaped slaves as part of the Underground Railroad.

Directly behind the Reeve house is the lower Friends Meeting House. Constructed in 1779 on land donated by Mark Reeve, it is an outstanding example of Colonial Quaker Meetinghouse architecture. The first trial of the alleged tea burners was held here in 1773 where, surprisingly, not one indictment was ever handed down in this land of patriots.

Today, of the many outbuildings that supported the home, tavern, hotel, and wharf, only this unsteady red barn remains. Since all outbuildings were most likely constructed of wood, several generations of them were built, rebuilt, and reutilized as the years wore on. The large wharf warehouse stood nearby until it too vanished by 1970.

THE VILLAGES OF DELAWARE WATER GAP

WALPACK, MILLBROOK, BEVANS, PETER'S VALLEY, AND FLATBROOKVILLE
SUSSEX & WARREN COUNTIES

For hundreds of square miles, the Delaware Water Gap National Recreation Area sprawls out on both sides of the River; to the east is New Jersey and to the West is Pennsylvania. Scenic vistas, quiet mountain roads, and 70,000 acres of mostly wilderness areas are all open to the public for their enjoyment. A visit today to the area on the Jersey side is a trip into a venerable time machine. The Old Mine Road, laid out by Dutch Miners in the 1660s remains the best way into the Gap on the New Jersey side. Here the narrow, crumbling road winds through the forest and occasional parking area for fishermen as it soon climbs deep into, first, Worthington State Forest and then eventually onto federal park property.

Along the roads are stone foundations, side by side with empty and forlorn buildings, vine covered houses, and the feeling that everyone just packed up and left. It wasn't always that way—not until about 1965, when a massive failed federal dam project bought out the residents of Pahaquarry and Walpack Townships in both Warren and Sussex Counties. The government had been planning since the August 1955 Delaware River floods, which caused massive damage to the area and was the result of heavy rain from two back-to-back Hurricanes Connie and Diane. It was during this flood that the first of the towns along the river would vanish: Brotzmanville, established all the way back in 1736; residents never rebuilt after the waters receded.

So, in an unsuccessful effort to control Mother Nature, a massive thirty-seven-mile-long reservoir was planned, today notoriously known as the Tocks Island Dam Project, which cast a spell on the area and still stings worse than a hornet some half a century later. The Army Corps of Engineers quickly bought out hundreds of people and destroyed homes, farms, and historic sites. As nothing could stand in the way of progress, the Dam would be built -- or so they thought anyway. After ten years of fierce opposition, the Army Corps left, turning the land and the villages that had escaped the wrecking ball over to the National Park Service. New Jersey Governors Cahill and Byrne were instrumental in blocking the project and in 1975, it was tabled; finally, in 2002, the project was officially abolished forever protecting what was left of this Valley's history and villages. In a 1995 *New York Times* interview, Virginia E. Fuller, then clerk of Walpack Township, recalled: "Everybody was very bitter about the whole thing because it turned life upside down".

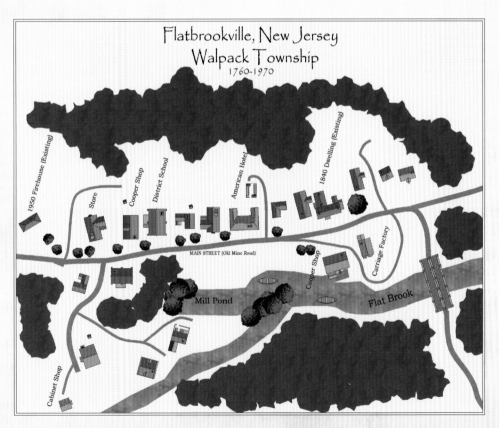

Flatbrookville, New Jersey
Walpack Township
1760-1970

1950 Firehouse (Existing)

Store

Cooper Shop

District School

American Hotel

1840 Dwelling (Existing)

MAIN STREET (Old Mine Road)

Carriage Factory

Cooper Shop

Mill Pond

Flat Brook

Cabinet Shop

Soon you will come to the c. 1899 truss bridge that has been closed for many years; the road was realigned to bypass the iron bridge. As soon as you cross the Flat Brook you will make a quick left turn onto Old Mine Road. Welcome to Flatbrookville, or in this case, welcome to what used to be Flatbrookville. It was here, around 1770, Benjamin Barton erected a gristmill along the banks of the Flat Brook, and in just a few years a village came to life. By 1820, Thomas Durling opened the first of three stores in the bustling hamlet, and the population continued to grow as new houses were built and business opened, including a spinning wheel factory.

By 1860, over $12,000 had been raised through subscriptions to build a bridge across the Delaware; however, it never came to fruition, and the little village continued to rely on the Rosencrans ferry to get to Pennsylvania. It was on November 21, 1828, that the US Post Office was authorized by President John Quincy Adams, and Jacob Smith was appointed the first postmaster. The rural post

Walpack native Elijah Rosencrans was born in the village on March 22, 1806, to Benjamin Rosencrans, a well-respected local farmer. Rosencrans carried on the farm life until 1854 when he moved to Flatbrookville. Upon his arrival in 1854, he constructed the American Hotel, rebuilt the mill, and built several houses in the town. For nearly thirty years he served as the justice of the peace and the tax assessor. A respected township leader, he lived a full and fruitful life, dying in 1885.

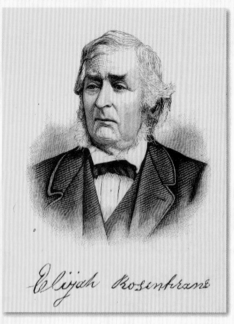

office operated for well over a century and was decommissioned on June 30, 1963. No trace of the post office exists today.

With the onset of the 1940s, Flatbrookville was no longer the center of commerce in the area, and the old American Hotel hadn't seen guests in years. The town slowly declined and was full of unpainted weathered buildings by the 1960s; though it still appeared on roadmaps well into the 1960s, it is doubtful many folks went there at all.

After the Army Corps debacle, nearly every structure in the village was bulldozed. Including the three-story American Hotel, the century-old homes, and once bustling stores, everything went except two buildings: the 1940s cinderblock firehouse and a single Greek revival 1840s residence. Main Street was gone in just a few days from the blade of a big Caterpillar bulldozer. Today, Main Street is a lonely, pot-holed road where not even the few could envision that a town stood here. Flatbrookville, which never had a population of more than 150, now has a population of probably about four and a whole bunch of wildlife!

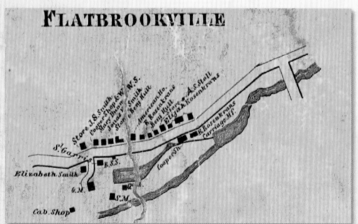

This 1860 map of Flatbrookville shows the busy village that it had grown into by the middle of the nineteenth century. Among the names of its residents were Rosencrans, Hull, Smith, and Garris. The village became the area's hub of stopping over, shopping, and industry.

The busy section of Old Mine Road that passed through the village was known locally as Main Street. Here the hotel, three stores, and various industries made for quite the busy place, all in the beautiful scenery of Delaware Water Gap.

Firehouse No. 2 of the Walpack Twp. Fire Department was completed in 1950. Previous to this time, Flatbrookville relied upon fire protection from Walpack Center or Belvidere. This small building is one of two buildings that remain in the village today; it has not housed fire apparatus in years.

The little iron bridge crossing the Flatbook hasn't been used in years. A new concrete span was erected by the county putting an end to the c. 1890s iron truss bridge's usefulness. It is similar to other bridges in the area and near identical to the Flatbrook-Roy Bridge in Walpack Center.

After the Army Corps of Engineers took possession of the lands in the Gap, they quickly went about leveling everything in sight. This photo was taken in the exact same spot as the previous one; today, no trace of a village exists. My wife thought we surely must have been on the wrong road, but we were not. Whatever buildings the Corps spared, the National Park Service razed in the 1980s.

The once-busy village of dozens of homes and stores has been reduced to just one house, albeit a beautiful one. It may be one of the fine Greek revivals that Elijah Rosencrans erected in 1854 near his store and hotel.

"Reading, riting and rith'matic" were once taught in this small schoolhouse constructed by the Township in 1874. Known as District School No. 18, it served until 1929 when it was converted into a rooming house. It was torn down by the National Park Service about 1978.

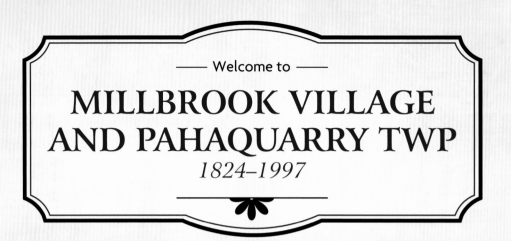
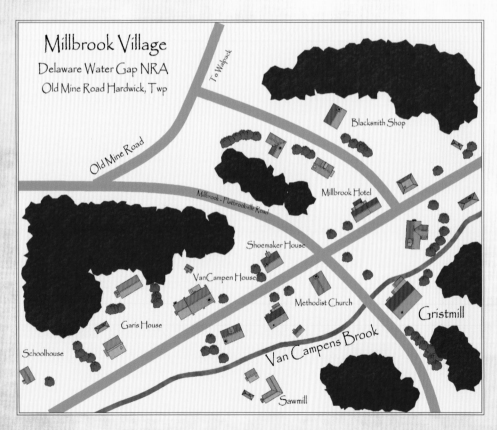

Millbrook Village

Delaware Water Gap NRA

Old Mine Road Hardwick, Twp

To Wallpack

Old Mine Road

Blacksmith Shop

Millbrook - Flatbrookville Road

Millbrook Hotel

Shoemaker House

VanCampen House

Methodist Church

Gristmill

Garis House

Van Campens Brook

Schoolhouse

Sawmill

HARDWICK TWP, WARREN COUNTY

Pahaquarry Township was formed on December 27, 1824, straddling the ridge along Van Campens Brook. Originally, part of Sussex County was deeded to Warren County at the time of its creation. The name "Pahaquarry" is from the Native American word "Pahaquarra," which was derived from "Pahaqualong," which meant to the Minisink's "the place between the mountains beside the waters." The Little village along the Old Mine Road drew settlers in from both Pennsylvania and New Jersey; by 1850, the principal village, known as Mill Brook, consisted of a sawmill, tannery, gristmill, and hotel, as well as a Methodist church and school. In 1860, the population of the township reached its peak with about 460 persons calling Pahaquarry and Mill Brook home. After 1880, the isolated village of Millbrook began to lose residents, by 1890, there were but 261 folks in the township,

One of the original buildings in the village is the schoolhouse, a typical one-room structure of rural educational design. However, the school was first built as the Methodist church in 1840, where school was conducted in the basement.

The mill that put the "mill" in Millbrook was established in 1832 by Abraham Garis along Van Campens Brook. Successful during its run of nearly seventy years, it closed its doors in 1900. In 1922, the long silent mill was destroyed by fire. The site sat empty until the early 1990s when this mill was found in Bartsonville, Pennsylvania. Disassembled and rebuilt in Millbrook, it since has been made fully operational. You see, it really isn't the mill that put the "mill" in Millbrook after all!

and in 1930, there were eighty. After the dam project in 1965, it was down to seventy-one and soon it became apparent that Pahaquarry and little Millbrook were fading into history.

In 1997, the last dozen or so people who called it home were annexed by neighboring Hardwick Township. So, today, little is left of Pahaquarry Township with the exception of the now-restored Mill Brook Village. About fifty percent of the place is original with the remainder having been relocated to the site to put Mill Brook back to represent rural village life in the mid-nineteenth century. Annually, Mill Brook Village Days are held to celebrate the community and the people who settled it. Christmas services are still held in the Methodist church and the restored mill looks as if it could go into operation tomorrow if need be.

When you leave Mill Brook and head west deeper into the woods the road continues to wind and follow the river. The next notable building you will come to is the former Pahaquarry Town Hall, which was originally the Calno District Schoolhouse and last saw students way back in 1940.

The National Park Service fully restored the 131-year-old schoolhouse in 1971, just one year after this photo was taken for the HABS. One of several early schools in Pahaquarry Township, it most likely ceased being used as a school in the 1930s. (The Library of Congress)

The school was moved to a new location in 1860 after the new Methodist church was built next door. This postcard from the early 1970s shows what life was like during a spring recess around 1900 in what was once District School #82.

Here, along the old Main Street of Millbrook, is the Garis House. It is typical of small one-and-one-half-story frame houses that dotted New Jersey's farms and villages in the nineteenth century. The 1880 book *The History of Warren County* described the area as "the most secluded township in the State."

When the new plans were designed for the replacement church in 1860, it was decided to greatly expand the building's footprint. The interior of the church is modest and has never been modernized, with the exception of electricity. Religious services are still held in the church around the huge pot-belly stove.

This blacksmith shop is a reproduction; however, it is a faithful recreation of this ever-busy village trade. A blacksmith is most well known for shoeing horses, but that was just a tiny slice of what they did. Building and repairing farm implements, wagon parts, household goods, stoves, and pretty much anything that was made of metal, a blacksmith could make or bring it to life again.

The earliest known view of Pahaquarry Township was made in February of 1794. In just a few years, Millbrook Village would be settled and become the principal town center in the Township. Starting in the late 1960s, the National Park Service began relocating historic structures to Millbrook from throughout the area. By 1985, relocated structures joined the original ones, and the village began to resemble its former 1870s self.

Another small village that once existed not far from Millbrook was Calno. A small hamlet of a dozen or so houses, there was also a post office and schoolhouse. When this school was later consolidated, it became the Pahaquarry Township Hall. The township dwindled to just eight residents by 1997 and soon merged with Hardwick Township ending its 173-year existence.

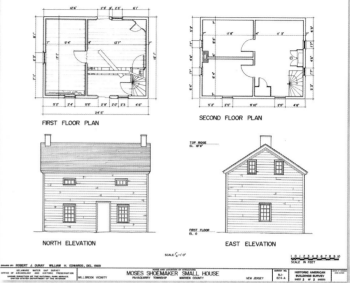

FIRST FLOOR PLAN

SECOND FLOOR PLAN

NORTH ELEVATION

EAST ELEVATION

MOSES SHOEMAKER SMALL HOUSE

Sometimes when conducting historical research, you will find that things just do not add up. The Shoemaker House was probably dated incorrectly at the time of the HABS and most likely dates to about 1815 or before; it was also listed as destroyed in 1973. It was, however, not destroyed—only moved and preserved at Millbrook Village for future generations to learn about the Tocks Island Dam nightmare.

With the government flood waters imminently rising to destroy the region's cultural and historical fabric, it was decided to document as many buildings as possible that would surely soon be destroyed. The Moses Shoemaker Farm was one such place, as was this small house found on the property. (The Library of Congress)

Once standing near the Delaware River, this hamlet was used by those crossing the river here, known as Shoemakers Eddy. At least two hotels and a few other buildings surrounded the farmstead. The ferry operation, begun in 1815, continued on until its last trip in 1938.

Welcome to
WALPACK CENTER
Settled 1828

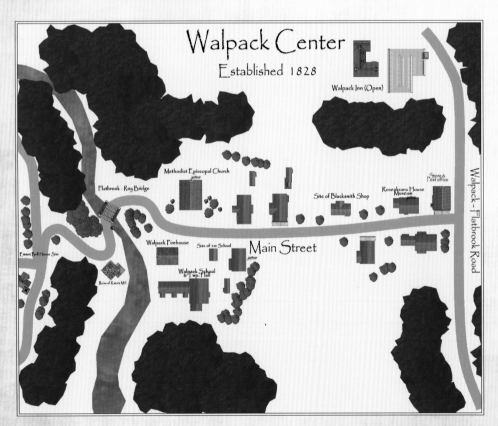

WALPACK TOWNSHIP, SUSSEX COUNTY

Heading back out to Old Mine Road, travel North to Walpack. Soon, the Walpack Inn will come into sight, a famed eating establishment that has been run by the Heigis family since 1967. Pass by the Inn and round the bend to find Main Street on the left. Welcome to beautiful, peaceful, and all but forgotten Walpack Center. Walpack Township itself can trace its establishment prior to 1731 when the first Dutch settlers migrated down from Newburgh, New York. Over the next century, the lands of Walpack comprised a huge section of this area, stretching all the way to the New York State line. The word "Walpack" itself is derived from the Delaware Indian name, "Wahl-Peck" meaning whirlpool in the river.

Just when the name Walpack was first used is not known; however, in 1828, the US Post Office took that name when it opened at a location most likely on the east side of the Flat Brook near the cemetery. Walpack Center was first known as Pleasant Valley, where a church and cemetery were established in 1837 also in the vicinity of the Flat Brook and Keen's Mill. Over the next decade, additional people moved into the fertile valley, and in 1850, Isaac and Jasper Rundle opened the first store on Main Street. That first store stood until 1915 when it was destroyed in a fire, although it was soon replaced by the present building. Walpack had no organized fire company in those days; however, a large soda acid fire extinguisher was kept across from the store that could be loaded onto a wagon when needed. It would not be until about 1930 when the Walpack Volunteer Fire Department was established. The first firehouse in town was, oddly enough, a cave that was dug into the side of the hill across from the store. Here some buckets, Indian tanks, and soda acid fire extinguishers were kept until a lightly used 1930 Model A Ford pumper arrived around 1940.

Main Street was lined with a variety of homes and buildings that were crucial to any village's function. Most of the original structures remain today, including the 1850 Rundle House, which today serves as headquarters for the Walpack Historical Society; this organization has worked hard for nearly thirty years to preserve the village. The Methodist church, constructed in 1872, at a cost of $7,000, is an architectural gem and replaced an earlier 1837 church by the cemetery. The Village Post Office still remains although only in part-time operation. The former 1893 schoolhouse has housed the Township Hall, its mayor, and two-member council, since the schools were consolidated with Sandyston Townships at the last day of school on June 14, 1951.

Walpack Center along with Millbrook, Bevans, and other areas, are part of the National Park Service's property. Of course, as with some ghost towns, a few folks hold on; there are about two dozen full-time residents living in Walpack township, along with some seasonal National Park Service employees from time to time, making this the least populated township in the most densely populated state.

Visitor Information

Visiting all the villages in the Delaware Water Gap are at least a full day for the average visitor. Although you will spend most of your time touring the seasonally opened buildings at Millbrook, or by chance at Walpack Center, the rest of time will be spent trying to figure out where you made the wrong turn thirty minutes ago! Old Mine Road twists and turns and doubles back on itself while its crossroads often have no street signs—the GPS will not know where you are most of them time, and modern maps have deleted some of the places in this area. A best bet for the serious explorer is to pick up a set of topographic maps of Warren and Sussex Counties to aide in your travels. If you are coming from the South, off Interstate 80, be prepared as there are absolutely no services (gas, food, etc.) unless you go to Blairstown. From I80, twenty-five really slow miles to the Layton General Store is a long time with no cold (or hot) beverage, so heed the warnings! I encourage you to call the National Park Service Visitor Center, (570) 828-6125, for information on events and closures before visiting. Like Sandy Hook, you could spend a day, or a lifetime, exploring the area and learning about the rich history of this mostly forgotten region of our state. Be sure to arrange dinner at the Walpack Inn, (973) 948-3890, for an evening of great food in this historic roadside treasure.

The Post Office, Wallpack Center, N. J.

The tranquil village of Walpack Center remains much as it did in this c. 1905 postcard view. The heart and soul of Walpack Township has endured against the odds for nearly two centuries. On the right is the first general store, which opened in 1850.

Walpack's Methodist Church was completed in 1871 replacing a small stone church located just over the Flatbrook-Roy Bridge. The Methodist congregation attended services weekly until 1978 when it became property of the National Park Service.

Rev P.E. WHITMORE 1907

M.E. Church Wallpack Centre N.J.

The thirty-foot high spire, which was once a landmark of the valley, was blown over and destroyed in a storm many years ago. The small hipped roof replacement is adequate, albeit inglorious for this country church.

Top: One of the most fascinating aspects of the church is the interior Frescos. Painted soon after the church was constructed to add depth and faux architectural detail inside, they once made the rather plain interior come alive. They were covered with wallboard sometime in the 1940s in an attempt to modernize the church, covering the Frescos. As time and money come available it is hoped that they will someday be restored.

Right: By 1890, the number of those needing an education had outgrown the old schoolhouse, which had been in use since the 1870s. A local contractor constructed a new larger building nearly next door to the old one and opened for the 1893–1894 school year.

Left: On June 14, 1951, the school locked its doors and turned the keys over to the township for use as the municipal building. For over a half-century, the old school has served as the Township Hall, where the Walpack Mayor and Council still meet to run the place.

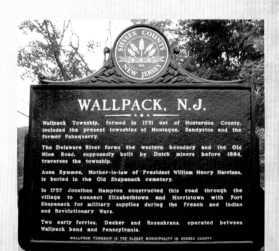

WALLPACK, N.J.

Wallpack Township, formed in 1731 out of Hunterdon County, included the present townships of Montague, Sandyston and the former Pahaquarry.

The Delaware River forms the western boundary and the Old Mine Road, supposedly built by Dutch miners before 1664, traverses the township.

Anna Symmes, Mother-in-law of President William Henry Harrison, is buried in the Old Shapanack cemetery.

In 1757 Jonathan Hampton constructed this road through the village to connect Elizabethtown and Morristown with Fort Shapanack for military supplies during the French and Indian and Revolutionary Wars.

Two early ferries, Decker and Rosenkrans, operated between Wallpack bend and Pennsylvania.

WALLPACK TOWNSHIP IS THE OLDEST MUNICIPALITY IN SUSSEX COUNTY

Walpack may be the only fire department in New Jersey, or even America, whose first firehouse was a cave. The department started in 1939 and soon received this donated 1933 Seagrave pumper from the City of Belleville. Belleville repainted and lettered the engine for Walpack and loaded it full of equipment, a kind gesture to get the boys ready to fight fire.

The village blacksmith shop was located on the west side of Main Street, about mid-way between the store and the Methodist church. I suspect that this building was the first Walpack School, which had been built in the 1850s and later recorded as becoming a blacksmith shop. It has long since vanished from the village.

Lee Rosencrans became the first fire chief in Walpack Township and was responsible for erecting the second firehouse across from the Methodist church in 1950. The two-bay firehouse held the department's 1933 Seagrave and 1929 Model A Ford pumpers. In 1955, the department took delivery of a brand new Mack B model pumper, which lasted until the fire department disbanded c. 1972.

Since I first photographed this gas pump next to the firehouse in 2011, someone has stolen the cover from it. Theft of historic items on National Park land can put you in jail quickly. It is hoped that someday it will be returned to the village.

Wallpack Center, N. J.

The once-busy corner of Main Street contained the entire business district in one building. Post office, store, gasoline filling station, and farm supplies could all be found in one place. The original store was destroyed in a 1915 fire, after which this building was erected. Since that time, several additions have been removed, leaving the Walpack Center Post Office and its lonely zip code of 07881 as the sole tenant.

Main Street seems to be suspended in time, free from traffic lights and the clutter of our busy modern lives. Aside from an occasional cyclist or National Park Service employee, not much happens in the village today, and that's just the way the remaining locals like it.

Keen's Mill once stood adjacent to the Flatbrook-Roy Bridge on the outskirts of the village. Constructed about 1830, the mill stood until the early twentieth century when it was lost to either flood or fire. The original grindstone still lies near the foundation of the mill as a proud reminder of the hard work and history of this place.

Just pass Keen's Mill stood the Emmet Bell House, a two-story dwelling built about 1825. The house was the site of many country auctions over the years, and generations of the Bell family were born and died in the house. It was destroyed by fire in the 1950s; its replacement also no longer exists.

The Flatbrook – Roy Bridge was constructed by the Groton Bridge Company in 1889 and has been rehabilitated several times since. In bridge design, it is a pony truss, one of thousands of prefabricated bridges that once spanned the creeks and rivers throughout America. They are quickly vanishing as progress marches on.

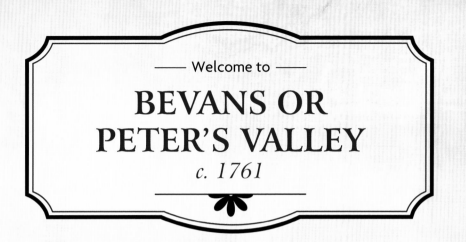

Welcome to
BEVANS OR PETER'S VALLEY
c. 1761

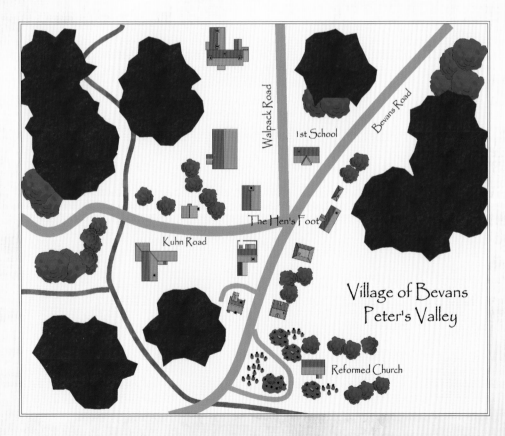

SANDYSTON TOWNSHIP, SUSSEX COUNTY

The last stop in the Gap is the Village of Bevans or Peter's Valley. This small hamlet is located at the crossroads where Walpack, Kuhn, and Bevans Road intersect in the rolling hills of Sandyston Township. Known as the Hen's Foot, this intersection has been called that for over 200 years by the locals. The general area in this vicinity has been known as Peter's Valley since 1761, when Peter VanNest first made his home alongside the Delaware. Within a few years, the village took shape, and new houses sprung up, along with two churches, a hotel, a school, and a mill.

It should be noted that VanNest was responsible for surveying most of the township's roads; ironically three of them came together directly in front of his residence! Both churches were completed in similar frame construction in 1838–1839; of these, the Universalist Church is today a private residence, while the Reformed Church is owned by the Park Service and used for events, including weddings, from time to time.

So, back to the Bevans-Peter's Valley debate. So what had been called Peter's Valley from 1761 or so took on a new identity when James Bevans became the postmaster of the village in 1829; through influence or just good timing he was able to apply for the post office as Bevans. Any historian can tell you that post office names change(d) with the wind—even to this day villages have names of post offices from other towns, names of towns that don't exist, and many of us get our mail from a post office other than the place we pay our taxes, too!

Edward A. Webb's *Historical Directory of Sussex County* (1872) described the place as such:

Store and Residence of Frank McKeeby, Bevans, N. J.

> Peter's Valley, or The Corners, as it is called, was named nearly a hundred years ago from Peter Van Nest. It is situated in the lower part of the township. The hotel is one of the oldest buildings in the place, it was originally built for a school house, and religious services were performed in it on the Sabbath. It was a building one and a half stories high, afterwards raised to two. It is now occupied as a hotel. The scenery from the hills surrounding the town is not surpassed by any in our county. A post office has been recently placed here called Bevans P.O. There is in the place a store, a blacksmith's shop, and two coopers' shops, besides the hotel.

Bevans continued, along with Layton, to be a primary village of Sandyston Township; the area was farmed and changed little over the first 200 years of its existence. Once again the Tocks Island Project chased many from their homes, and by 1969, Bevans was just another Water Gap ghost town. This was all about to change with the creation of the Peter's Valley craft center created by the National Park Service in 1970. For decades, the buildings have been leased to this cooperative, which has existed to further the disciplines of blacksmithing, ceramics, fiber surface design, fiber structure, fine metals, photography, special topics and woodworking, according to their brochure. The craft center has undoubtedly kept Bevans uniquely alive when so many other places like Flatbrookville and Brotzmanville have vanished entirely.

The Bevans Store and Post Office was most likely established about 1829 at the intersection known as the Hen's Foot. It remained in operation as an active store until closing in 1969 because of the impending dam waters about to arrive. However, they didn't arrive, and in the mid 1970s, the place was crafted into the Peters Valley Craft Center by the National Park Service.

The graveyard of the Dutch-reformed church in the village is filled with settlers, veterans, and many headstones bearing the town's namesake: Bevans. Our old cemeteries are where those who have built this nation and protected it now repose. They are peaceful places to and throughout our great state; many ancient ones await your research and preservation to keep them respectful.

In 2010, the Sandyston Township Historical Commission erected this sign to bring attention to the village of Bevans. This often overlooked village remains an important part of Sussex County Heritage, and thanks to those who created the Peter's Valley Craft Village, which has prospered for nearly a half century. Only by a little luck and a bit of government confusion, this area does not lie at the bottom of the failed reservoir project.

BEVANS, NEW JERSEY

Originally named for early settler and surveyor Peter Van Neste in 1761. Nicknamed Hen's Foot, The Corners, and finally Bevans for its Postmaster James C. Bevans in 1829. The Peter's Valley Society for Literature was est. Jan. 1, 1813. The Dutch Reformed Church at Peter's Valley was built in 1838. The Universalistic Church was gathered in 1847. The historic "Old Mine Road" and Delaware River are to the West. Peter's Valley flouring mill ruins on the Big Flatbrook lie nearby. Bevans was lost to the Tocks Island Dam Project of 1960-70's and the name Peter's Valley was reinstated. Today this hamlet and surrounding area belong to the National Park Service.

DONATED BY SANDYSTON TOWNSHIP HISTORICAL SOCIETY - 2010

CONCLUSION

Without a doubt, putting this book together became both an adventure and an in-depth lesson of our state's geography, architecture, and history. Of the dozens of villages that have vanished or been forgotten about, it is impressive that so many were directly responsible for contributing to and ensuring the success of our new nation during the American Revolution. We might take for granted that we have per square mile more ghost towns and forgotten crossroads then any of the other forty-nine states; they are here for all of us to explore, photograph, and create our own history as we weave them into our lives and memories. From the Rocky ridges of Northwest, to the forests of the Pines and onto the golden sands of the Jersey Shore, these places are just waiting for you to arrive and take advantage of all they have to offer.

Personally, creating this book allowed such a great insight into places that I thought I knew oh so well and affirmed what a special place New Jersey truly is to visit and to those who call it home. This book was nearly eight years in the making, starting in 2008 with the mission to get to every ghost town throughout Jersey. With the completion of this book, I am able to share that journey with you and sincerely hope that you set out on your own for an adventure upon the roads less traveled.

BIBLIOGRAPHY

Beck, Henry Charlton. *Forgotten Towns of Southern New Jersey*. (New Brunswick, NJ: Rutgers UP, 1983).

Beck, Henry Charlton. *Jersey Genesis; the Story of the Mullica River*. (New Brunswick: Rutgers UP, 1945).

Beck, Henry Charlton. *More Forgotten Towns of Southern New Jersey*. (New Brunswick: Rutgers UP, 1963).

Bolger, William. *Smithville: The Result of Enterprise*. (Mount Holly, NJ: Commission, 1980).

Boucher, Jack E. *Of Batsto and Bog Iron*. (Batsto, NJ: Batsto Citizens Advisory Committee, 1964).

Cast Iron Soil Pipe & Fittings Handbook, Chapter 1, Cast Iron Soil Pipe History, Uses and Performance. *Cast Iron Soil Pipe & Fittings Handbook, Chapter 1, Cast Iron Soil Pipe History, Uses and Performance*. N.p., n.d. Web. 06 July 2016.

Chen, David W. "Six People Away From a Ghost Town; Pahaquarry, New Jersey's Tiniest Municipality, Tries to Disappear." *New York Times* [New York] 27 Oct. 1995, Region sec.: n. page. Print.

Ewing, Sarah W. R. *Atsion: A Town of Four Faces*. (Batsto, NJ: Batsto Citizens Committee, 1979).

Ewing, Sarah W. R. *An Introduction to Batsto*. (Batsto, NJ: Batsto Citizens Committee, 1986).

Giles, John R. *The Story of Waterloo Village: From Colonial Forge to Canal Town*. History, n.d. Print.

Gordon, Thomas Fitzhugh. *A Gazetteer of the State of New Jersey . . . The History of New Jersey*. (Trenton: Daniel Fenton, 1834).

Kobbé, Gustav. *The Jersey Coast and Pines; an Illustrated Guide-book with Road Maps*. (Baltimore: Gateway, 1970).

Kopczynski, Susan. "Ride Down Old Mine Road Part I: Worthington State Forest to Watergate." *Spanning the Gap* 22 No. 2 (Oct. 2012): n. pag. Print. The newsletter of Delaware Water Gap National Recreation Area

McCloy, James F., and Ray Miller. *The Jersey Devil*. (Wallingford, PA: Middle Atlantic, 1976).

McMahon, William. *South Jersey Towns: History and Legends*. (New Brunswick: Rutgers UP, 1973).

Merwin, Daria E. "The Potential for Submerged Prehistoric Archaeological Sites off Sandy Hook." *Bulletin of the Archaeological Society of New Jersey* (2003): n.p. Print. Department of Anthropology State University of New York at Stony Brook Stony Brook, New York 11794-4364

Moss, George H. *Nauvoo to the Hook; the Iconography of a Barrier Beach*. (Locust, NJ: Jervey Close, 1964).

National Park Service/U.S. Department of the Interior / Gateway National Recreation Area. *Sandy Hook Lighthouse*. N.p.: National Park Service/US Department of the Interior / Gateway National Recreation Area, n.d. Print.

"Phalanx Blaze Puts an End to Efforts to save House." *Red Bank Register* 15 Nov. 1972: n. pag. Web.

Pierce, Arthur D. *Iron in the Pines: The Story of New Jersey's Ghost Towns and Bog Iron*. (New Brunswick, NJ: Rutgers UP, 1957).

Plunges, Gregory J. *Story of Phalanx*. (Freehold: Monmouth County Historical Society, 1980).

Sickler, Joseph S., and Charles Cordrey. *Tea Burning Town: Being the Story of Ancient Greenwich on the Cohansey in West Jersey*. (New York: Abelard, 1950).

Sitkus, Hance Morton. *Allaire*. (Charleston, SC: Arcadia, 2002).

Smith, Samuel Stelle. *Sandy Hook and the Land of the Navesink*. (Monmouth Beach, NJ: P. Freneau, 1963).

Snook, Myra. *Early Schools in Walpack Township*. (Walpack, NJ: Walpack Historical Society, 2007).

Solem-Stull, Barbara. *Batsto Village: Jewel of the Pines*. (Plexus, 2014).

Solem-Stull, Barbara. *Ghost Towns and Other Quirky Places in the New Jersey Pine Barrens*. (Medford: Plexus Pub., 2005).

Westergaard, Barbara. *New Jersey, a Guide to the State*. (New Brunswick: Rutgers UP, 1987).

Williams, Robert, and Mary Christman. *Over the Mountain: A Place Called Walpack*. (Walpack, NJ: Walpack Historical Society, 1988).

Woodward, Carl Raymond. *Ploughs and Politics: Charles Read of New Jersey and His Notes on Agriculture, 1715 - 1774*. (Philadelphia: Porcupine, 1974).

Yates, Willard R. *Joseph Wharton: Quaker Industrial Pioneer*. (Bethlehem: Lehigh UP, 1987).

INDEX

ABOUT THE AUTHOR

New Jersey historian and writer **Timothy Regan** is a lifelong resident of Monmouth County, with exception of three short years living the good life in Texas and Mississippi. Tim has been immersed in the history of New Jersey for as long as he can remember, thanks to his parents Betty and Gene, who were both always sharing, remembering, and preserving the past. His love of ghost towns began with his family's weekend trips in a big blue Chevy Impala, bouncing along the back roads to places like the Deserted Village of Allaire. By 1983, he became one of three youngest members of the Keyport Historical Society. In the decades that followed, Regan traveled around the state and published ten books on New Jersey history, wrote numerous articles, and contributed to the preservation and protection of Fort Hancock. He is also the founder and past director of the Keyport Fire Museum. Regan has served as the chief of both the Keyport Fire Department and the Sandy Hook Fire Department, where on October 29, 2012, he became the last permanent resident since 1764 to leave Sandy Hook, while evacuating for Hurricane Sandy. Regan resides in Monmouth County with his wife, Patti, and daughter, Elizabeth.